EASY GUITAR
WITH NOTES & TAB

2ND Edition

THE BEST OF JOHNNY CASH

T0045122

Cover photo by Tamara Reynolds, courtesy of the HOUSE OF CASH.

ISBN 978-0-7935-7585-5

HAL•LEONARD®
CORPORATION

7777 W. BLUEMOUND RD. P.O. BOX 13819 MILWAUKEE, WI 53213

Visit Hal Leonard Online at
www.halleonard.com

All Over Again

Words and Music by Johnny R. Cash

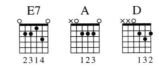

*Capo 1

Strum Pattern: 4
Pick Pattern: 3

Intro
   Moderately, in 2

*Optional: To match recording, place capo at 1st fret.

Verse

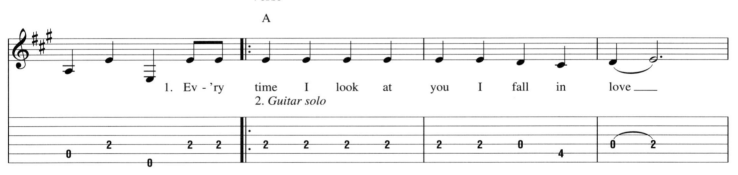

1. Ev - 'ry   time   I   look   at   you   I   fall   in   love ____
2. *Guitar solo*

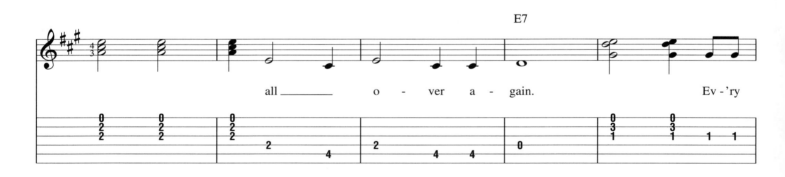

all _____ o - ver a - gain.   Ev - 'ry

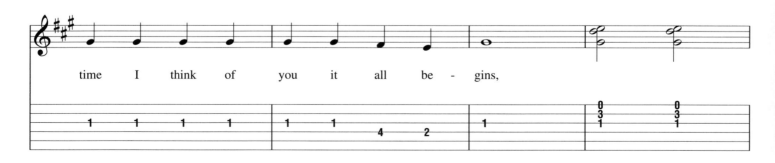

time   I   think   of   you   it   all   be - gins,

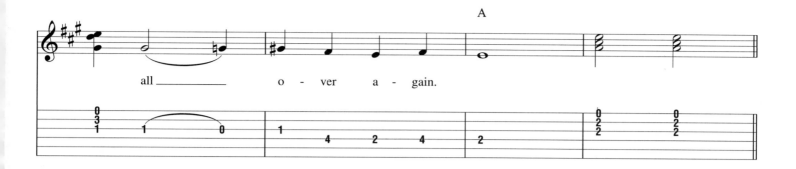

all _____ o - ver a - gain.

Bridge

One lit - tle dream at night and I can dream all day. It

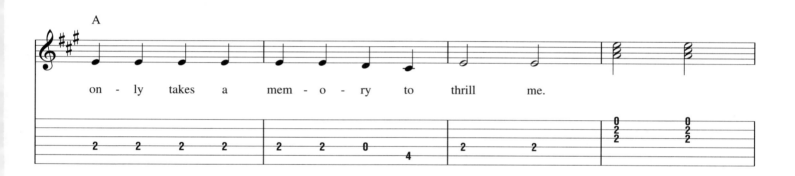

on - ly takes a mem - o - ry to thrill me.

One lit - tle kiss from you and I just fly a - way.

Pour me out your love un - til you fill me. I

Outro

want to fall in love be - gin - ning from the start

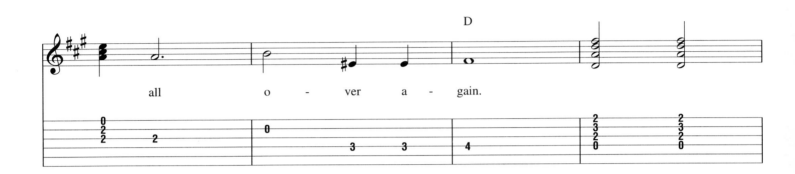

all o - ver a - gain.

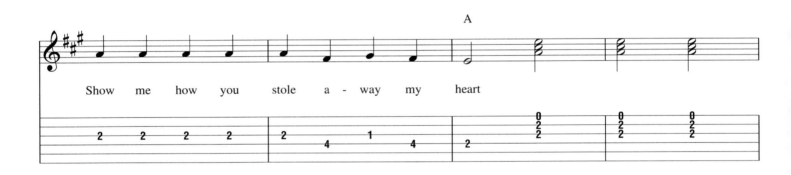

Show me how you stole a - way my heart

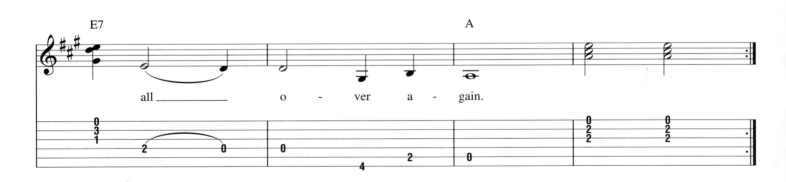

all _____ o - ver a - gain.

Repeat and fade

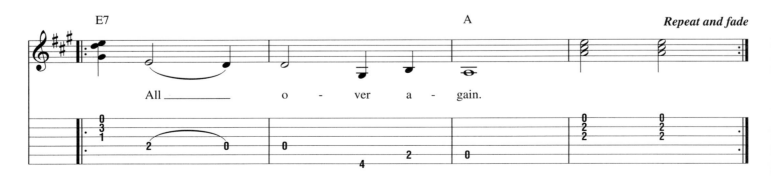

All _____ o - ver a - gain.

Big River

Words and Music by John R. Cash

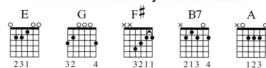

*Capo I

Strum Pattern: 4, 5
Pick Pattern: 1

Intro
Moderately, in 2

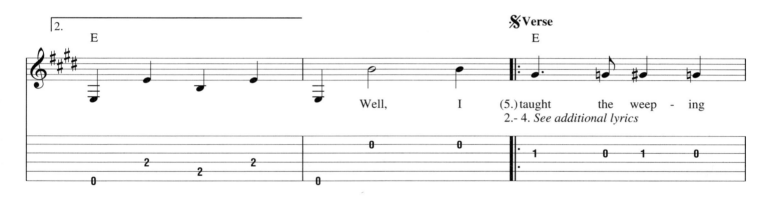

*Optional: To match recording, place capo at 1st fret.

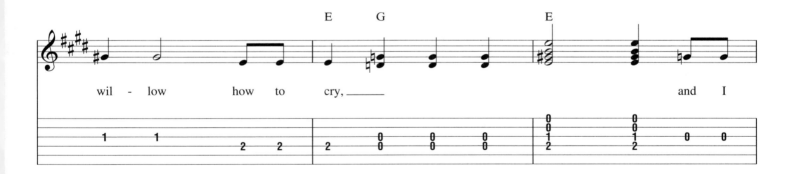

Well, I (5.)taught the weep-ing
2.- 4. *See additional lyrics*

wil - low how to cry, _____ and I

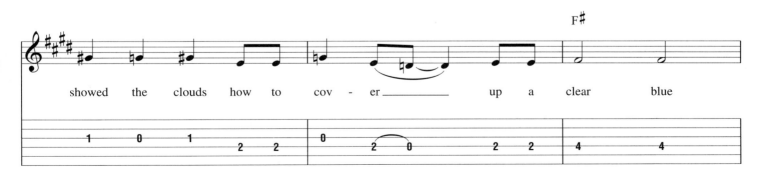

showed the clouds how to cov - er _____ up a clear blue

sky. And the tears that I cried for that wom - an _____ are gon - na

flood you, Big Riv - er. Then I'm gon - na sit right

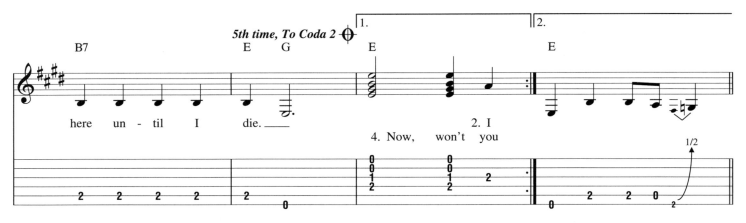

here un - til I die. _____

2. I
4. Now, won't you

Interlude

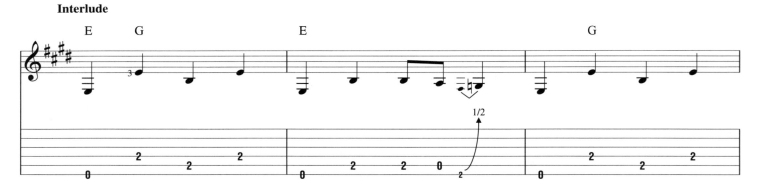

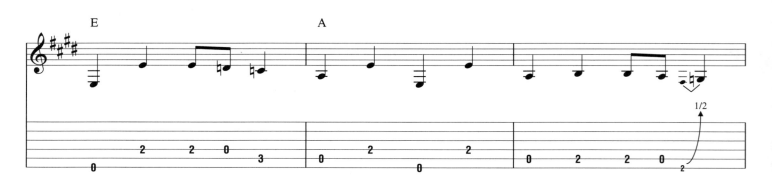

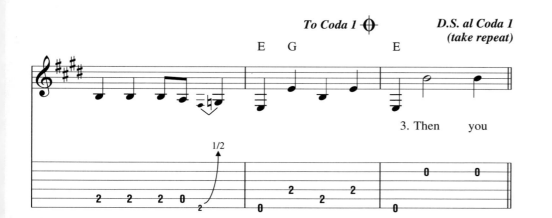

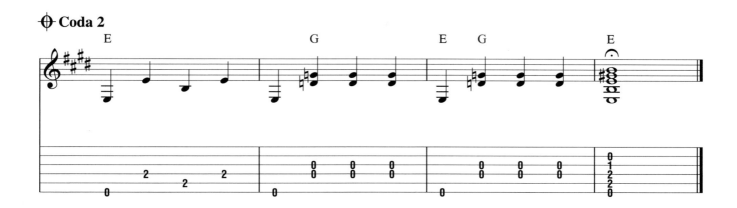

Additional Lyrics

2. I met her accidentally in St. Paul, Minnesota,
   And it tore me up ev'ry time I heard her drawl, southern drawl.
   Then I heard my dream was back downstream cavortin' in Davenport,
   And I followed you, Big River, when you called.

3. Then you took me to St. Louis later on, down the river.
   A freighter said, "She's been here, but she's gone, boy she's gone."
   I found her trail in Memphis, but she just walked up the bluff.
   She raised a few eyebrows, and then she went on down alone.

4. Now, won't you batter down by Baton Rouge, River Queen, roll it on.
   Take that woman on down to New Orleans, New Orleans.
   Go on, I've had enough; dump my blues down in the gulf.
   She loves you, Big River, more than me.

A Boy Named Sue

Words and Music by Shel Silverstein

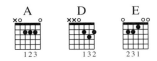

*Capo I

Strum Pattern: 4
Pick Pattern: 3

Intro   **Verse**

Moderately, in 2

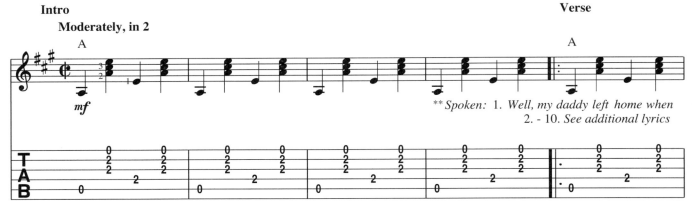

Spoken: 1. *Well, my daddy left home when*
2. - 10. *See additional lyrics*

*Optional: To match recording, place capo at 1st fret.   **Lyrics in italics are spoken throughout.

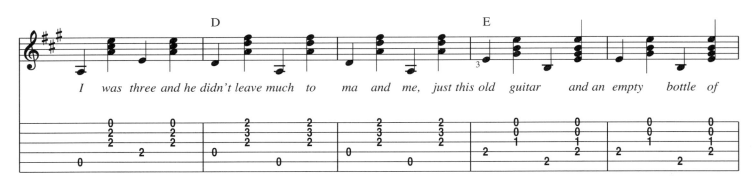

I was three and he didn't leave much to ma and me, just this old guitar and an empty bottle of

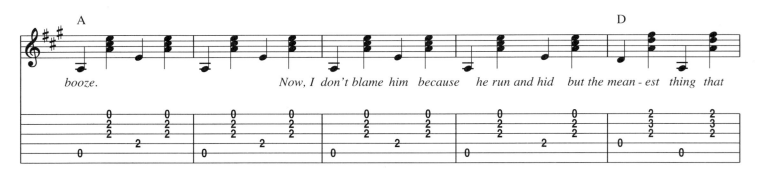

booze.   Now, I don't blame him because he run and hid but the mean-est thing that

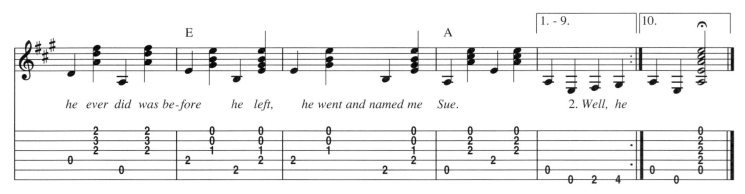

he ever did was be-fore he left, he went and named me Sue.   2. Well, he

2. *Well, he must have thought it was quite a joke,*
   And it got lots of laughs from a lots of folks.
   It seems I had to fight my whole life through.
   Some gal would giggle and I'd get red,
   And some guy'd laugh and I'd bust his head.
   I tell you, life ain't easy for a boy named Sue.

3. *Well, I grew up quick and I grew up mean;*
   My fist got hard and my wits got keen.
   Roamed from town to town to hide my shame,
   But I made me a vow to the moon and stars
   I'd search the honky-tonks and bars
   And kill that man that give me that awful name.

4. *Well, it was Gatlinburg in mid July,*
   And I had just hit town and my throat was dry.
   I'd thought I'd stop and have myself a brew.
   At an old saloon on a street of mud,
   There at a table dealing stud,
   Sat the dirty, mangy dog that named me Sue.

5. *Well, I knew that snake was my own sweet dad*
   From a worn-out picture that my mother'd had.
   And I know that scar on his cheek and his evil eye.
   He was big and bent and gray and old,
   And I looked at him and my blood ran cold,
   And I said, "My name is Sue. How do you do?
   Now you're gonna die." Yeah, that's what I told him.

6. *Well, I hit him hard right between the eyes,*
   And he went down, but to my surprise
   He come up with a knife and cut off a piece of my ear.
   But I busted a chair right across his teeth.
   And we crashed through the wall and into the street,
   Kicking and a-gouging in the mud
   And the blood and the beer.

7. *I tell you, I've fought tougher men,*
   But I really can't remember when.
   He kicked like a mule and he bit like a crocodile.
   I heard him laughin' and then I heard him cussin';
   He went for his gun and I pulled mine first.
   He stood there looking at me and I saw him smile.

8. *And he said, "Son, this world is rough,*
   And if a man's gonna make it, he's gotta be tough.
   And I know I wouldn't be there to help you along.
   So I give you that name and I said, 'Goodbye';
   I knew you'd have to get tough or die.
   And it's that name that helped to make you strong."

9. *"Yeah," he said, "Now you have just fought one helluva fight,*
   And I know you hate me and you've got the right
   To kill me now and I wouldn't blame you if you do.
   But you ought to thank me before I die
   For the gravel in your guts and the spit in your eye,
   Because I'm the son-of-a-bitch that named you Sue."

10. *Yeah, what could I do, what could I do?*
    I got all choked up and I threw down my gun,
    Called him a pa and he called me a son.
    And I come away with a different point of view.
    And I think about him now and then,
    Every time I tried, every time I win.
    And if I ever have a son, I think I am gonna name him
    Bill or George–anything but Sue.

Busted

Words and Music by Harlan Howard

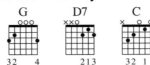

Strum Pattern: 8
Pick Pattern: 8

Intro
Slowly, in 2

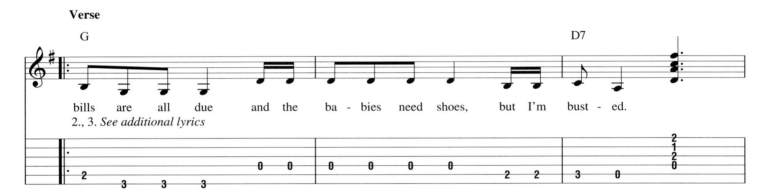

1. My

Verse

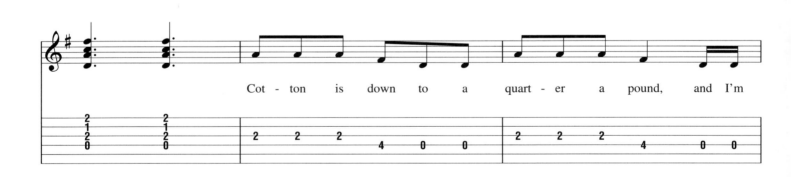

bills are all due and the ba - bies need shoes, but I'm bust - ed.
2., 3. See additional lyrics

Cot - ton is down to a quart - er a pound, and I'm

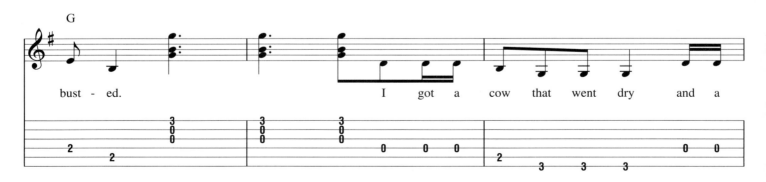

bust - ed.   I got a cow that went dry and a

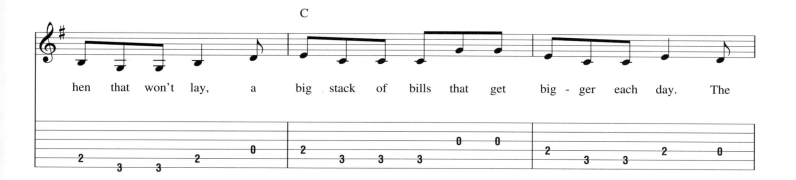

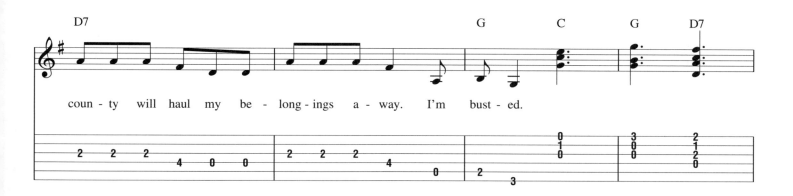

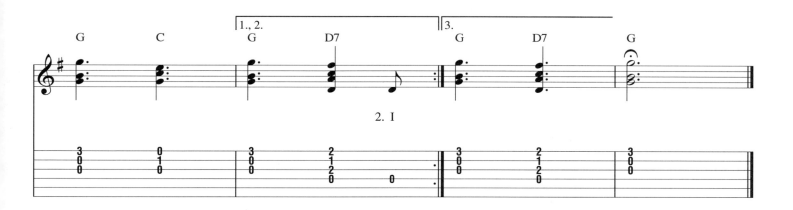

Additional Lyrics

2. I went to my brother to ask for a loan; I was busted.
   I hate to beg like a dog for a bone, but I'm busted.
   My brother said there ain't a thing I can do,
   My wife and my kids are all down with the flu,
   And I was just thinkin' of callin' on you, I'm busted.

3. Lord, I'm no thief, but a man can go wrong when he's busted.
   The food that we canned last summer is gone, and I'm busted.
   The fields are all bare and the cotton won't grow.
   Me and my fam'ly gotta pack up and go.
   Where I'll make a livin', the Lord only knows, but I'm busted.

Cry, Cry, Cry

Words and Music by John R. Cash

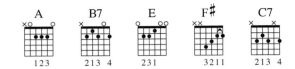

*Capo 1

Strum Pattern: 3
Pick Pattern: 3

Intro
Moderately, in 2

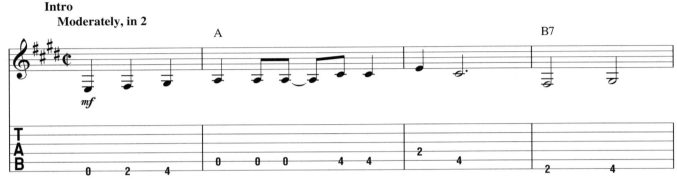

*Optional: To match recording, place capo at 1st fret.

℠ Verse

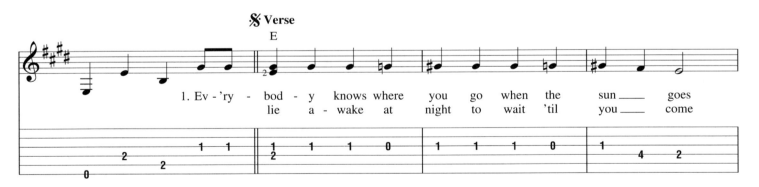

1. Ev-'ry-bod-y knows where you go when the sun ___ goes down. I think you on-ly live to see the lights up-

lie a-wake at night to wait 'til you ___ come in. You stay a lit-tle while and then you're gone a-

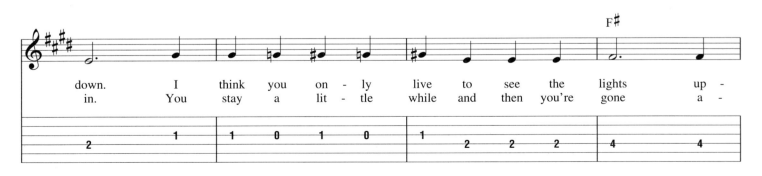

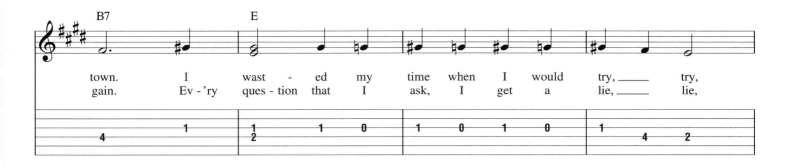

town. I wast-ed my time when I would try, _____ try,
gain. Ev-'ry ques-tion that I ask, I get a lie, _____ lie,

try, 'cause when the lights __ have lost their glow, __ you'll cry, cry, _____ cry.
lie. For ev-'ry lie __ you tell, you're gon-na cry, cry, _____ cry.

Verse

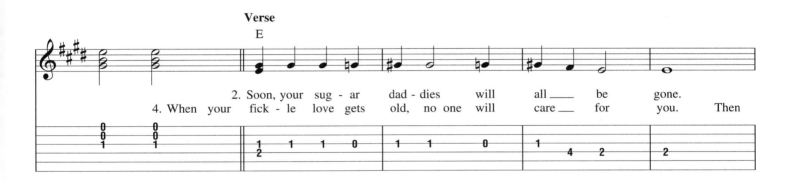

2. Soon, your sug-ar dad-dies will all ____ be gone.
4. When your fick-le love gets old, no one will care ____ for you. Then

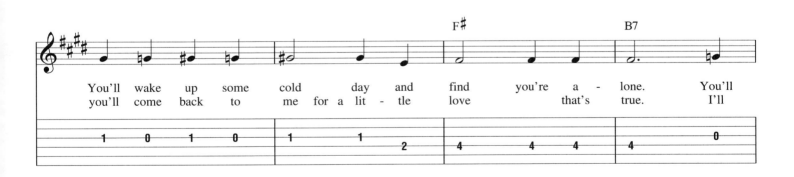

You'll wake up some cold day and find you're a - lone. You'll
you'll come back to me for a lit - tle love that's true. I'll

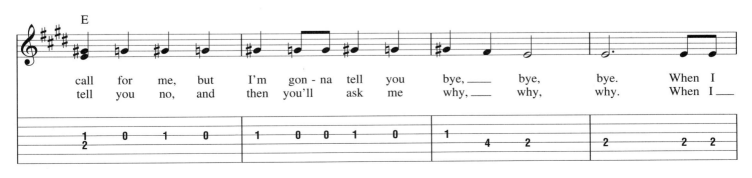

call for me, but I'm gon-na tell you bye, _____ bye, bye. When I
tell you no, and then you'll ask me why, _____ why, why. When I ____

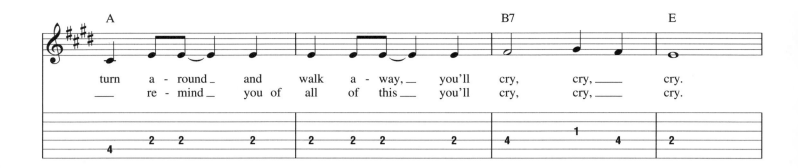

turn a- round_ and walk a - way, __ you'll cry, cry, ____ cry.
__ re- mind _ you of all of this __ you'll cry, cry, ____ cry.

Chorus

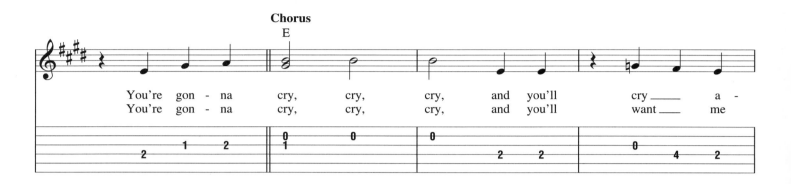

You're gon - na cry, cry, cry, and you'll cry ____ a -
You're gon - na cry, cry, cry, and you'll want ____ me

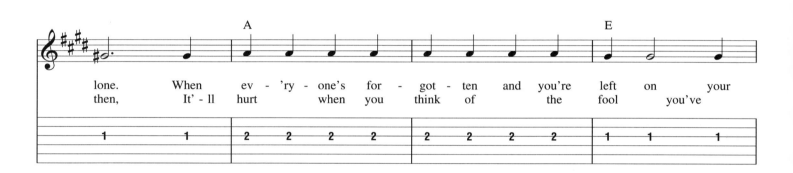

lone. When ev - 'ry - one's for - got - ten and you're left on your
then, It' - ll hurt when you think of the fool on you've

To Coda ⊕

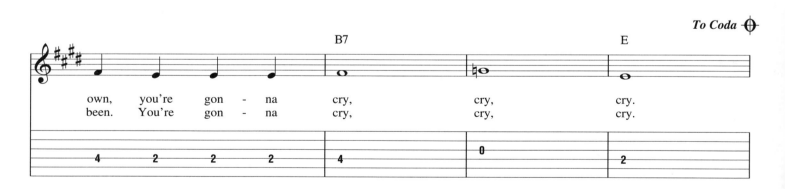

own, you're gon - na cry, cry, cry.
been. You're gon - na cry, cry, cry.

Interlude

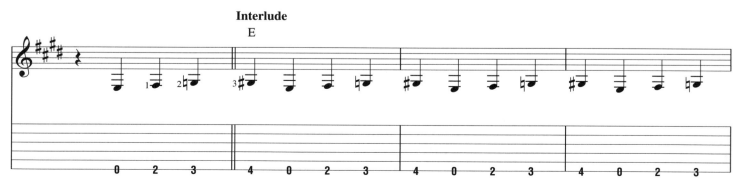

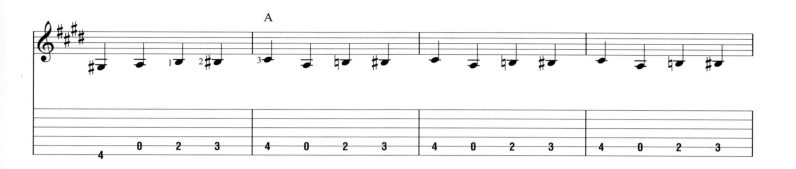

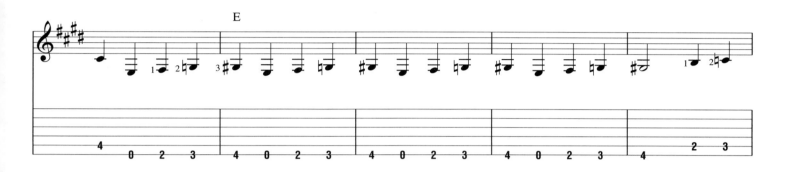

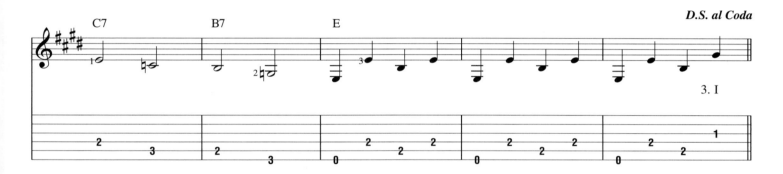

D.S. al Coda

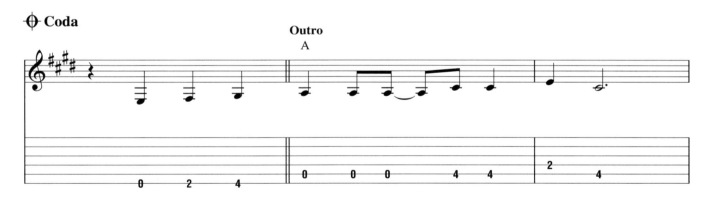

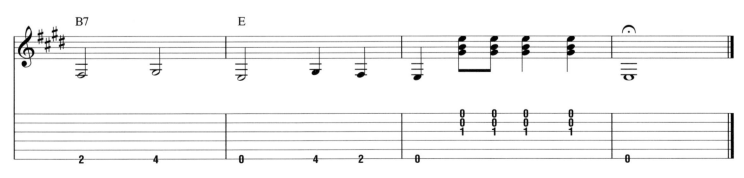

Daddy Sang Bass

Words and Music by Carl Perkins

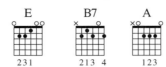

Strum Pattern: 3, 5
Pick Pattern: 1, 3

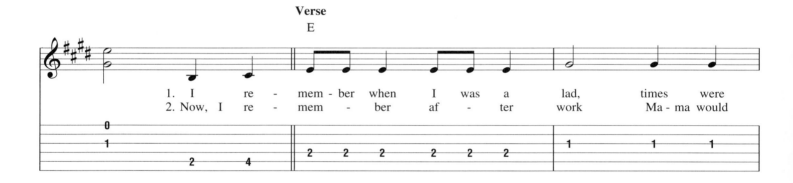

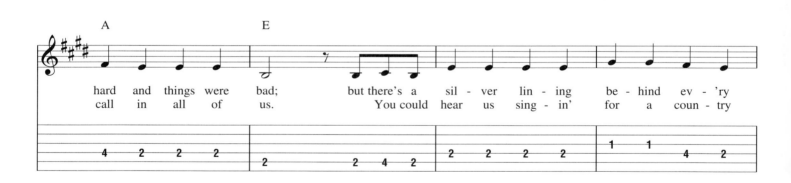

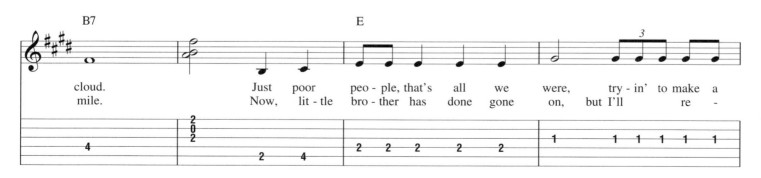

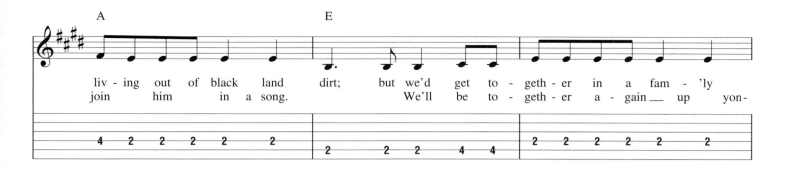

liv - ing out of black land dirt; but we'd get to - geth - er in a fam - 'ly
join him in a song. We'll be to - geth - er a - gain___ up yon-

Chorus

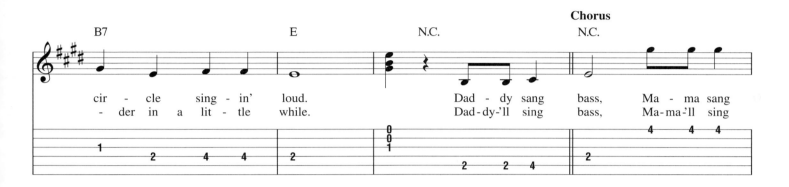

cir - cle sing - in' loud. Dad - dy sang bass, Ma - ma sang
- der in a lit - tle while. Dad - dy -'ll sing bass, Ma - ma -'ll sing

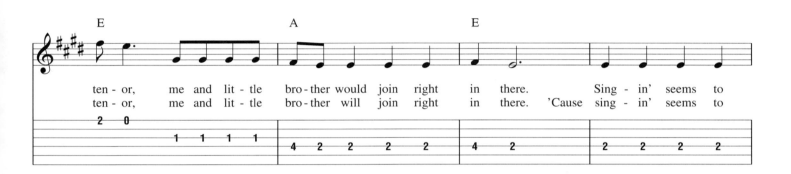

ten - or, me and lit - tle bro - ther would join right in there. Sing - in' seems to
ten - or, me and lit - tle bro - ther will join right in there. 'Cause sing - in' seems to

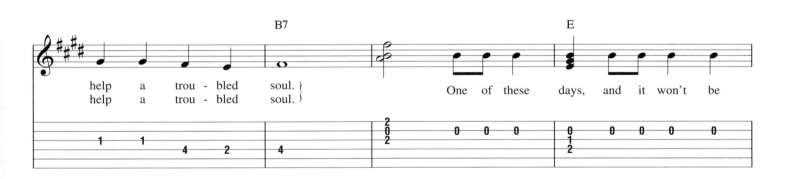

help a trou - bled soul. } One of these days, and it won't be
help a trou - bled soul. }

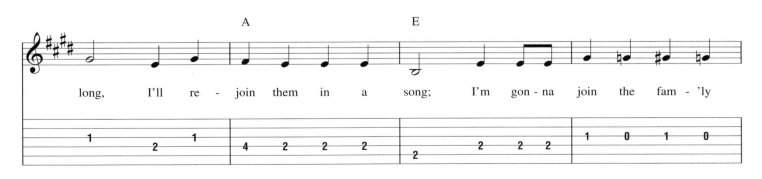

long, I'll re - join them in a song; I'm gon - na join the fam - 'ly

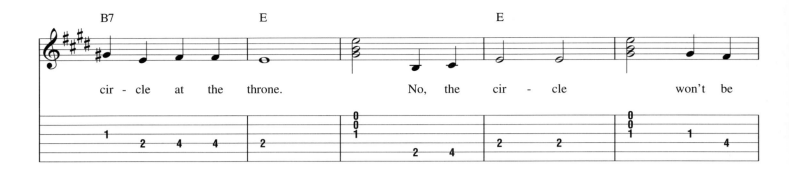

cir - cle at the throne. No, the cir - cle won't be

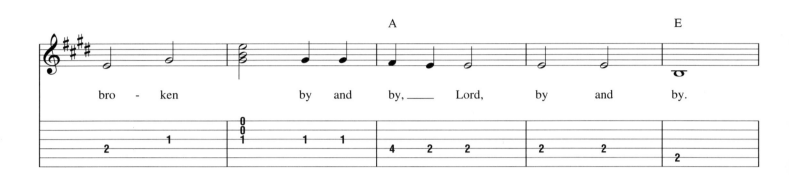

bro - ken by and by, ___ Lord, by and by.

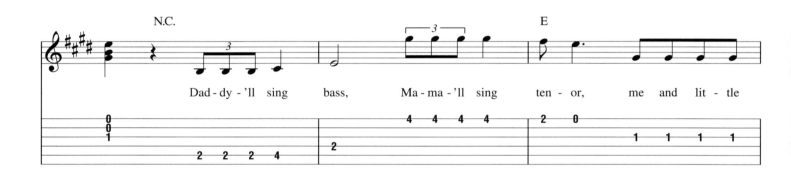

Dad - dy - 'll sing bass, Ma - ma - 'll sing ten - or, me and lit - tle

bro - ther will join right in there, in the sky, Lord, ___ in the sky.

In the sky, Lord, ___ in the sky.

Folsom Prison Blues

Words and Music by John R. Cash

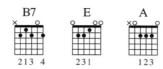

*Capo I
Strum Pattern: 4
Pick Pattern: 3

Intro
Moderately, in 2

*Optional: To match recording, place capo at 1st fret.

℅ Verse

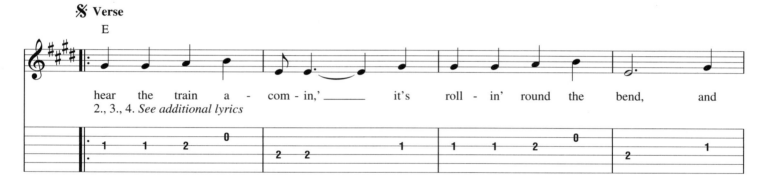

hear the train a - com - in,' _____ it's roll - in' round the bend, and
2., 3., 4. *See additional lyrics*

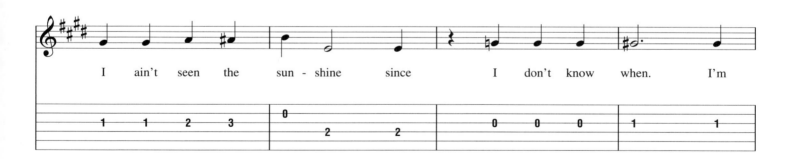

I ain't seen the sun - shine since I don't know when. I'm

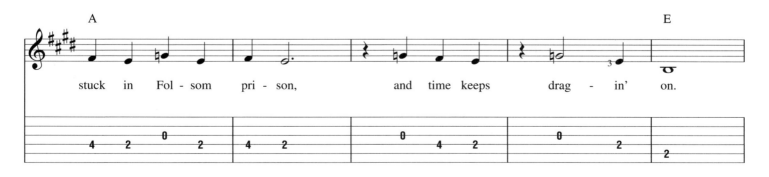

stuck in Fol - som pri - son, and time keeps drag - in' on.

But that train keeps a -

4th time, To Coda 2

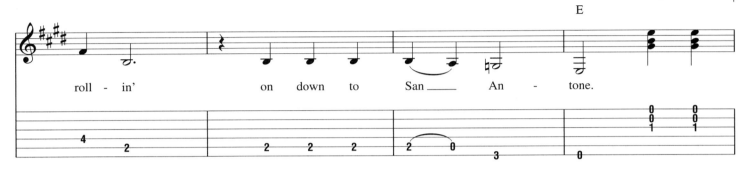

roll - in'   on down to San _____ An - tone.

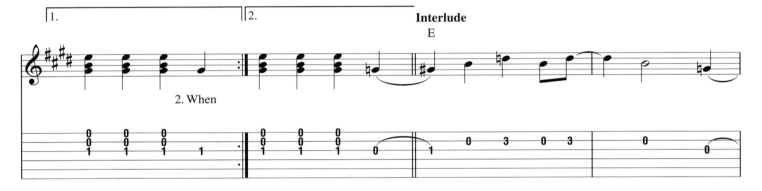

Interlude

2. When

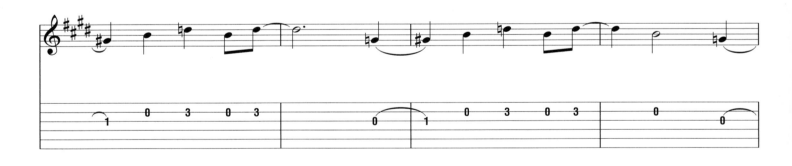

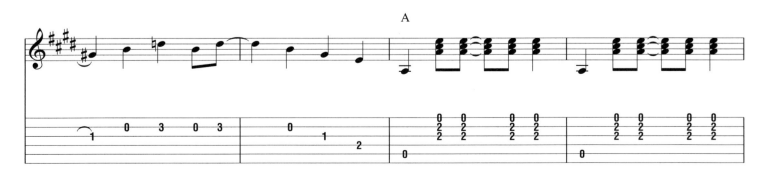

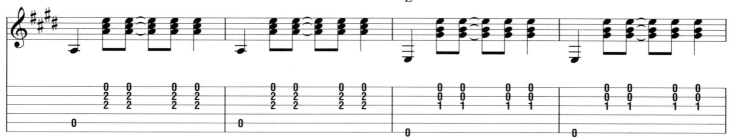

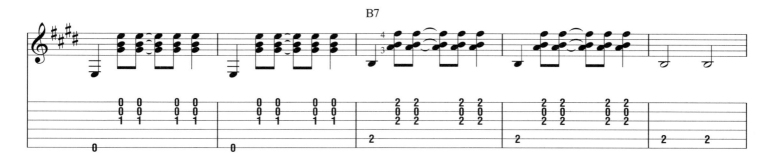

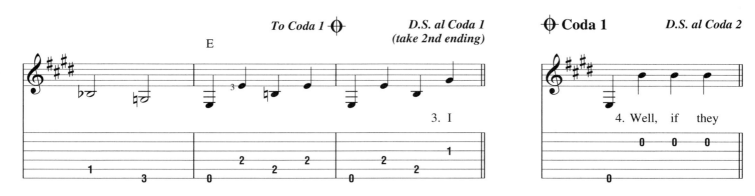

Additional Lyrics

2. When I was just a baby, my mama told me, "Son,
   Always be a good boy, don't ever play with guns."
   But I shot a man in Reno just to watch him die.
   When I hear that whistle blowin', I hang my head and cry.

3. I bet there's rich folks eatin' in a fancy dining car.
   They're prob'ly drinkin' coffee and smokin' big cigars.
   Well, I know I had it comin'. I know I can't be free.
   But those people keep a movin' and that's what tortures me.

4. Well, if they freed me from this prison,
   If that railroad train was mine,
   I bet I'd move it on a little farther down the line,
   Far from Folsom prison, that's where I want to stay.
   And I'd let that lonesome whistle blow my blues away.

Don't Take Your Guns to Town

Words and Music by Johnny R. Cash

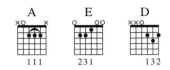

*Capo I

Strum Pattern: 3
Pick Pattern: 3

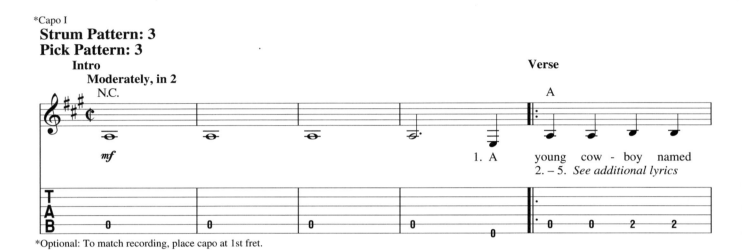

*Optional: To match recording, place capo at 1st fret.

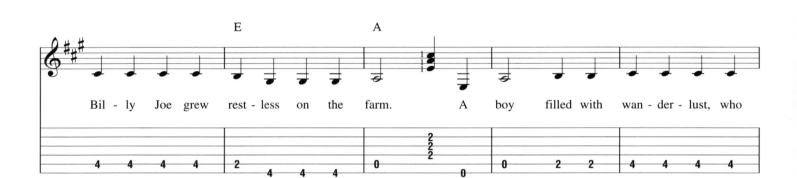

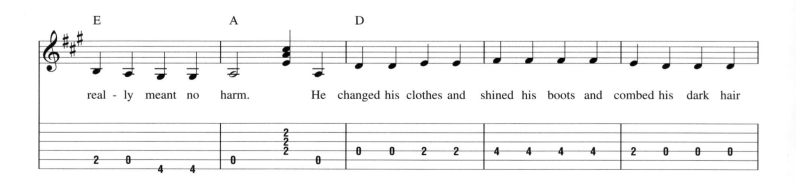

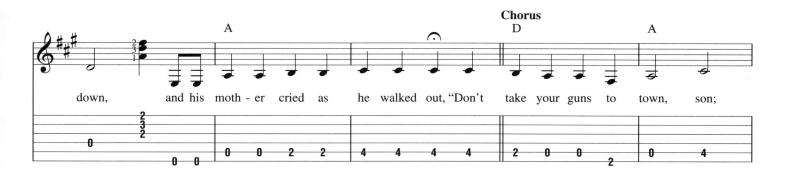

down, and his moth-er cried as he walked out, "Don't take your guns to town, son;

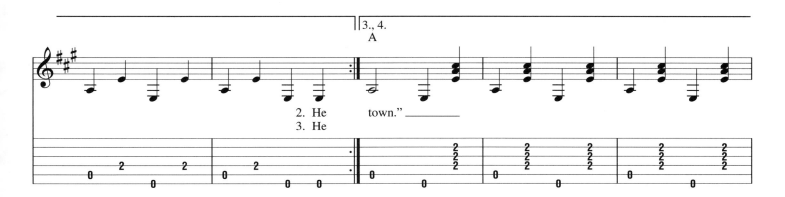

leave your guns at home, Bill. Don't take your guns to town." _____

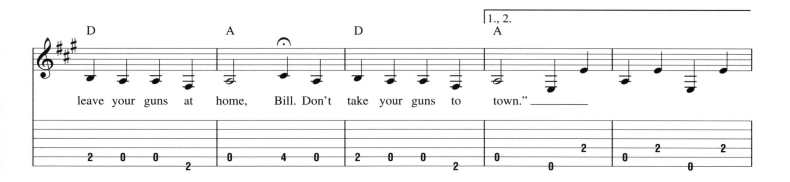

2. He town." _____
3. He

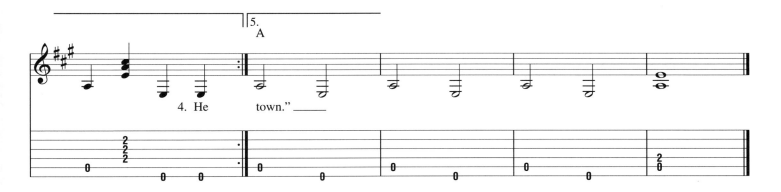

4. He town." _____

Additional Lyrics

2. He laughed and kissed his mom and said, "Your Billy Joe's a man.
I can shoot as quick and straight as anybody can.
But I wouldn't shoot without a cause; I'd gun nobody down."
But she cried again as he road away,

3. He sang a song as on he rode, his guns hung at his hips.
He rode into a cattle town, a smile upon his lips.
He stopped and walked into a bar and laid his money down.
But his mother's words echoed again:

4. He drank his first strong liquor then to calm his shaking hand
And tried to tell himself at last he had become a man.
A dusty cowpoke at his side began to laugh him down.
And he heard again his mother's words:

5. Bill was raged, then Billy Joe reached for his gun to draw.
But the stranger drew his gun and fired it before he even saw.
As Billy Joe fell to the floor, the crowd all gathered 'round,
And wondered at his final words:

Flesh and Blood

Words and Music by John R. Cash

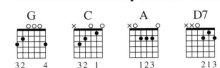

*Capo II

Strum Pattern: 3
Pick Pattern: 2, 3

Intro
Moderately, in 2

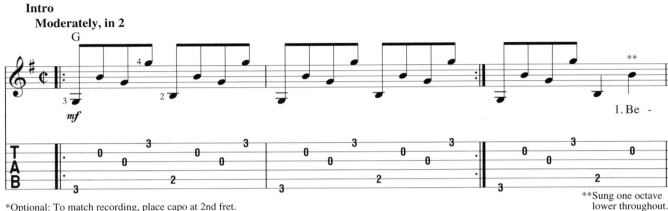

*Optional: To match recording, place capo at 2nd fret.

**Sung one octave lower throughout.

%︎ Verse

***

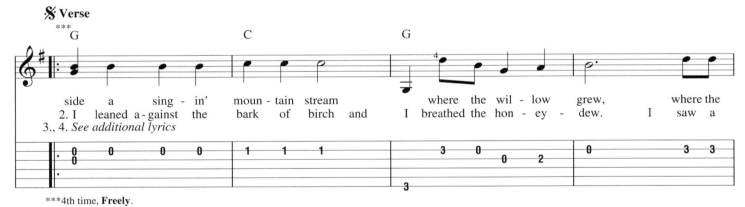

side a sing- in' moun- tain stream   where the wil- low   grew,   where the
2. I leaned a- gainst the   bark of birch and   I breathed the hon- ey- dew.   I saw a
3., 4. *See additional lyrics*

***4th time, **Freely**.

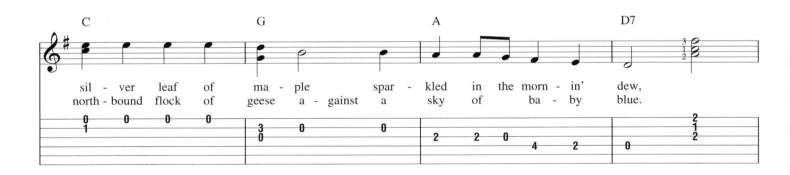

sil- ver leaf of   ma- ple   spar- kled in the morn- in'   dew,
north- bound flock of   geese a- gainst a   sky of ba- by   blue.

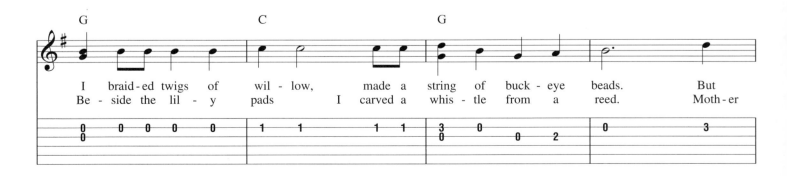

I braid- ed twigs of   wil- low,   made a   string of buck- eye   beads.   But
Be- side the lil- y   pads   I carved a   whis- tle from a   reed.   Moth- er

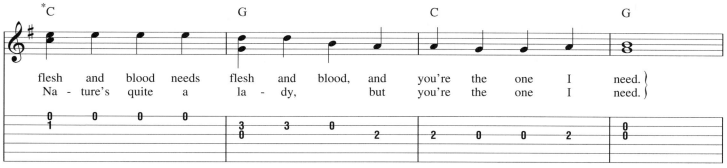

*4th time, **A tempo**.

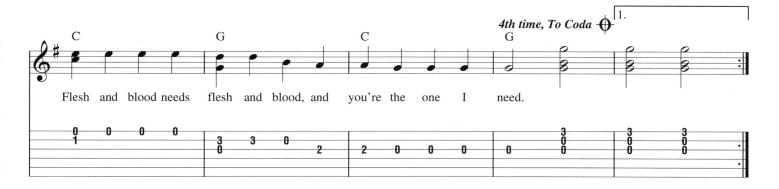

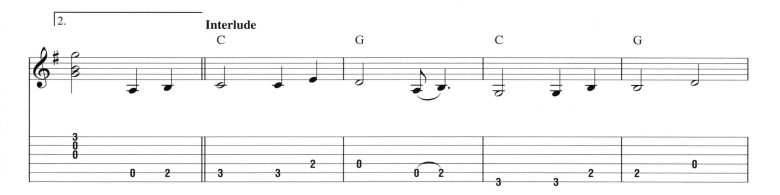

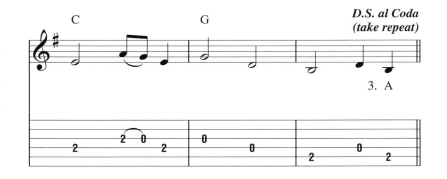

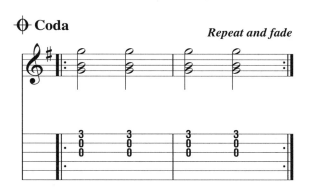

Additional Lyrics

3. A cardinal sang just for me and I thanked him for the song.
   Then the sun went slowly down the west and I had to move along.
   These were some of the things on which my mind and spirit feed.
   But flesh and blood needs flesh and blood, and you're the one I need.
   Flesh and blood needs flesh and blood, and you're the one I need.

4. So, when the day was ended I was still not satisfied,
   For I knew ev'rything I touched would wither and would die.
   And love is all that will remain and grow from all these seeds.
   Mother Nature's quite a lady, but you're the one I need.
   Flesh and blood needs flesh and blood, and you're the one I need.

Guess Things Happen That Way

Words and Music by Jack Clement

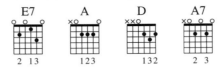

*Capo 1

Strum Pattern: 3

Pick Pattern: 3

*Optional: To match recording, place capo at 1st fret.

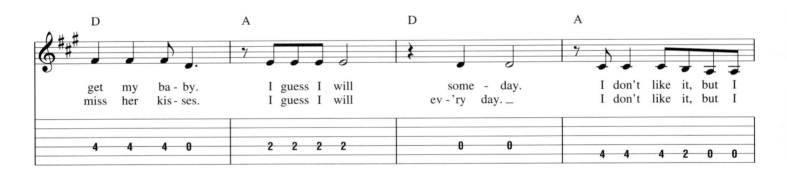

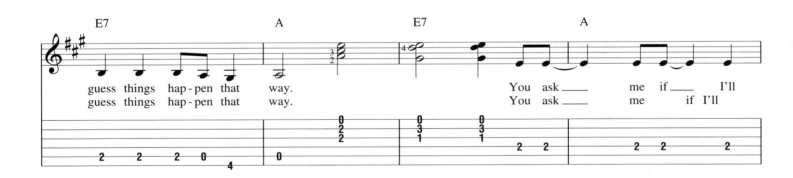

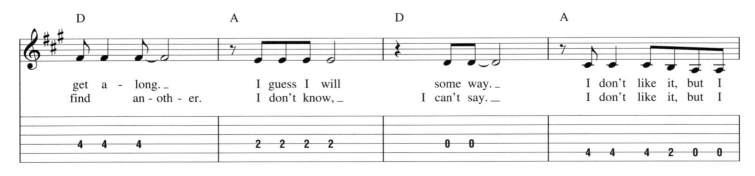

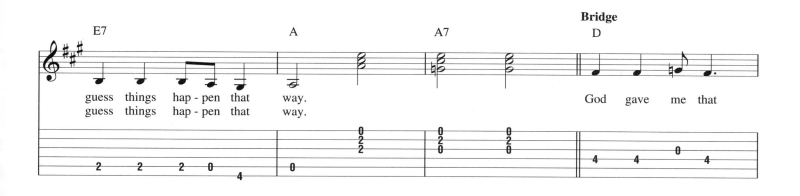

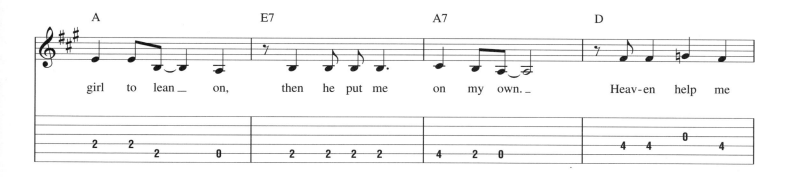

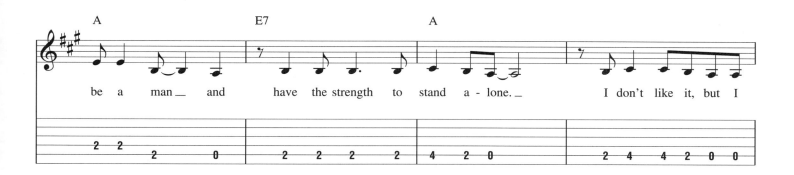

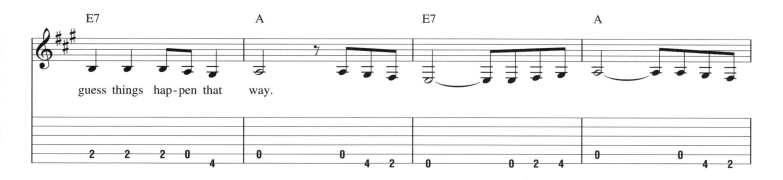

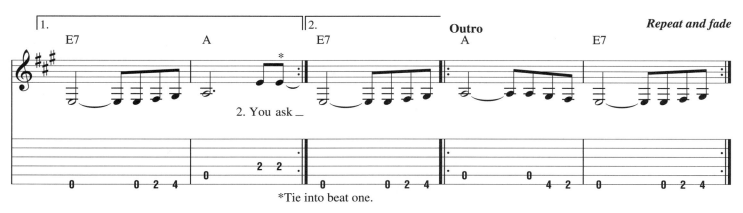

*Tie into beat one.

Hey, Porter

Words and Music by John R. Cash

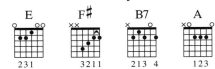

*Capo I

Strum Pattern:
Pick Pattern:

Intro
Moderately, in 2

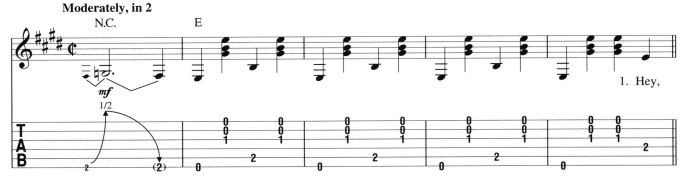

1. Hey,

*Optional: To match recording, place capo at 1st fret.

𝄋 **Verse**

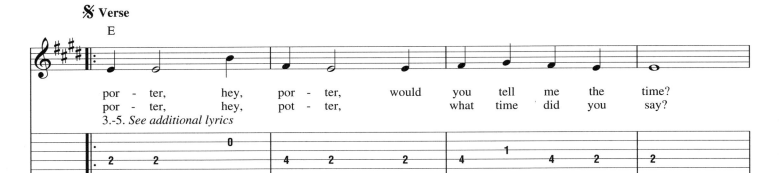

por - ter, hey, por - ter, would you tell me the time?
por - ter, hey, pot - ter, what time did you say?
3.-5. *See additional lyrics*

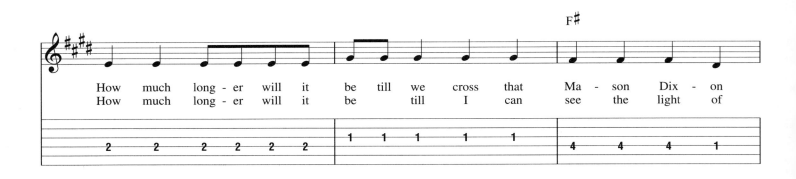

How much long - er will it be till we cross that Ma - son Dix - on
How much long - er will it be till I can see the light of

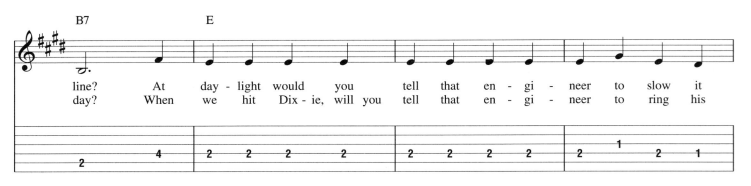

line? At day - light would you tell that en - gi - neer to slow it
day? When we hit Dix - ie, will you tell that en - gi - neer to ring his

down? Or bet - ter still, just stop the train, 'cause I want to look a -
bell, and ask ev - 'ry - bod - y that ain't a - sleep to stand right up and

To Coda 2

round.
yell?

2. Hey,

Interlude

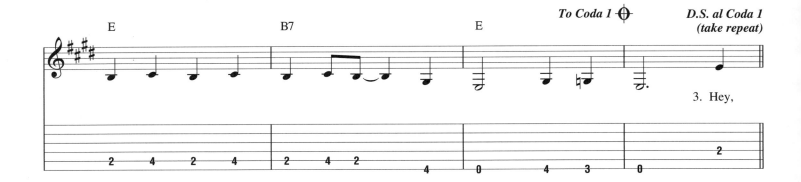

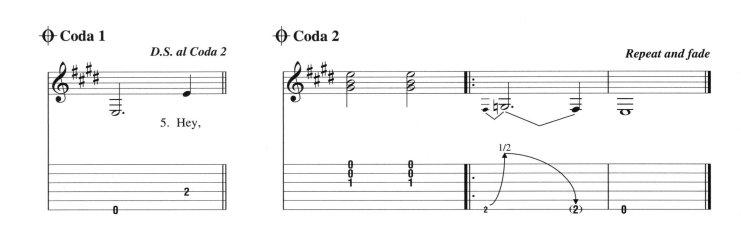

Additional Lyrics

3. Hey, porter, hey, porter, it's gettin' light outside.
   This old train is puffin' smoke and I have to strain my eyes.
   But ask that engineer if he will blow his whistle please,
   'Cause I smell frost on cotton leaves, and I feel that southern breeze.

4. Hey, porter, hey, porter, please get my bags for me.
   I need nobody to tell me now that we're in Tennessee.
   Go tell that engineer to make that lonesome whistle scream.
   We're not so far from home, so take it easy on the steam.

5. Hey, porter, hey, porter, please open up the door.
   When they stop this train, I'm gonna get off first 'cause I can wait no more.
   Tell that engineer I said, "Thanks a lot, and I didn't mind the fare."
   I'm gonna set my feet southern soil and breathe that southern air.

It Ain't Me Babe

Words and Music by Bob Dylan

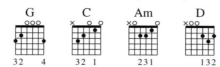

Strum Pattern: 3
Pick Pattern: 3

Intro

Moderately, in 2

*Harmonica arr. for gtr., next 12 meas.

Verse

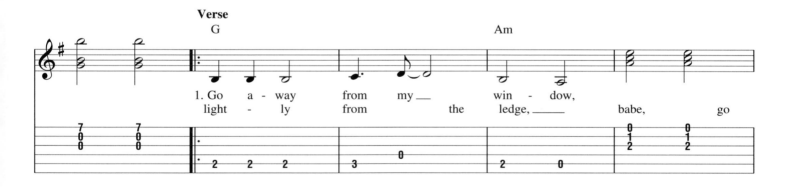

1. Go a - way from my ___ win - dow,
light - ly from the ledge, ___ babe, go

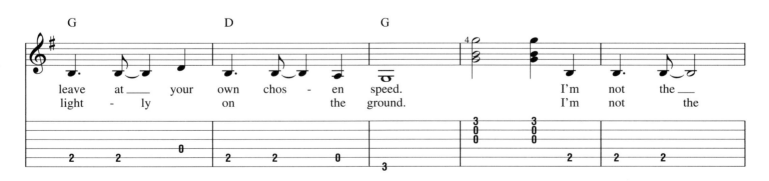

leave at ___ your own chos - en speed. I'm not the ___
light - ly on the ground. I'm not the

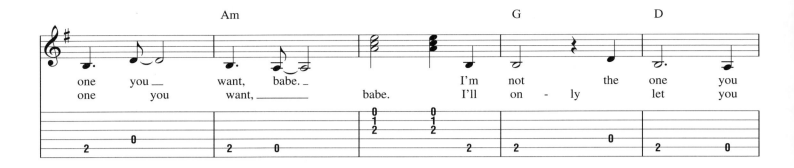

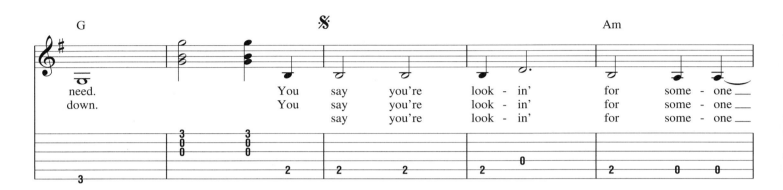

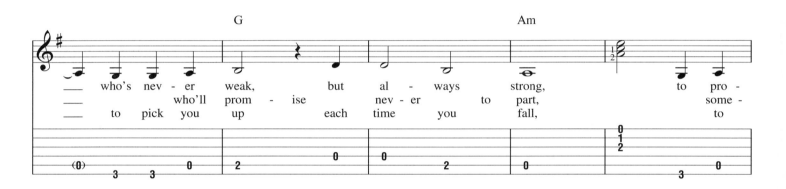

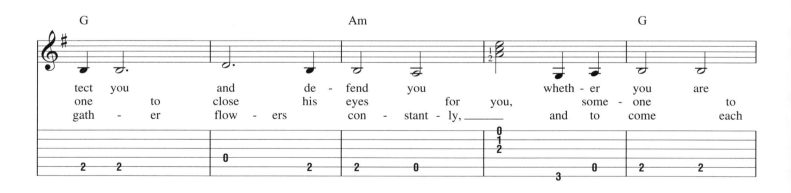

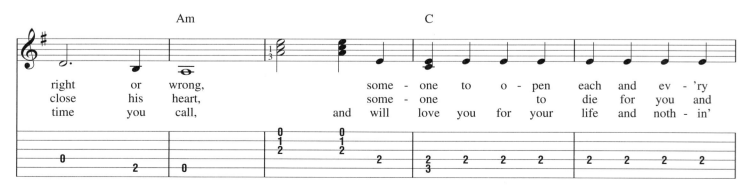

Chorus

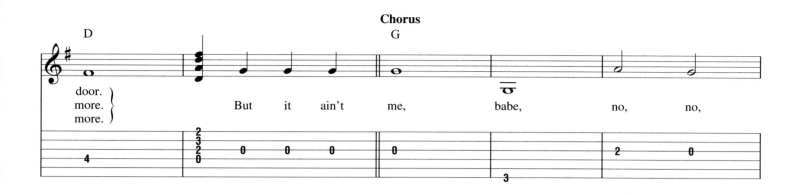

door.
more. } But it ain't me, babe, no, no,
more. }

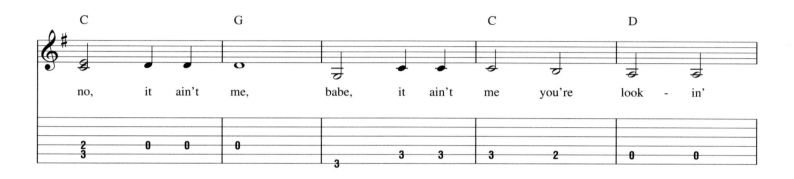

no, it ain't me, babe, it ain't me you're look - in'

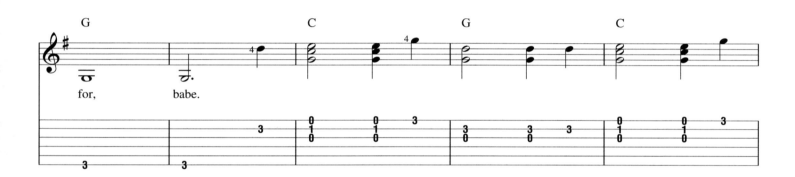

for, babe.

To Coda ⊕

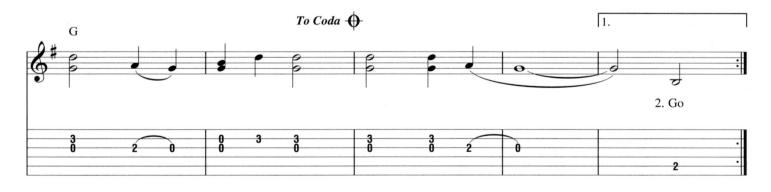

1.

2. Go

2.

D.S. al Coda

⊕ **Coda**

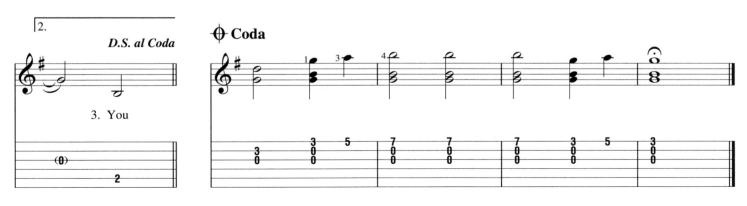

3. You

I Walk the Line

Words and Music by John R. Cash

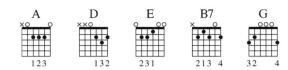

*Capo I

Strum Pattern: 3, 5
Pick Pattern: 5

Intro
Moderately, in 2

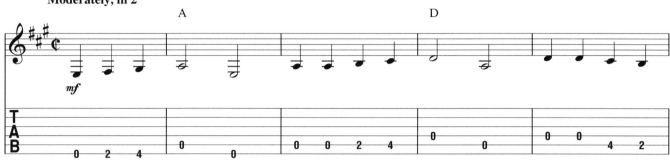

*Optional: To match recording, place capo at 1st fret.

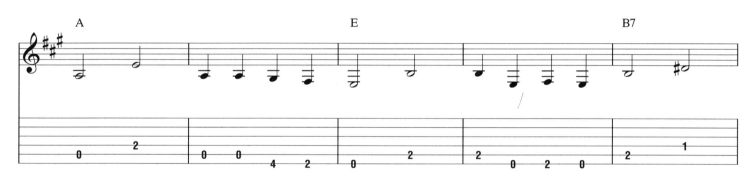

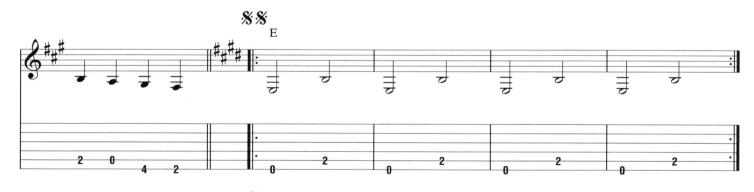

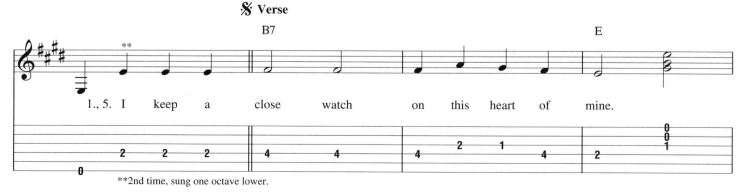

1., 5. I keep a close watch on this heart of mine.

**2nd time, sung one octave lower.

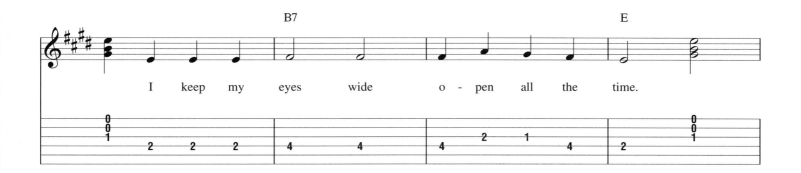

I keep my eyes wide o-pen all the time.

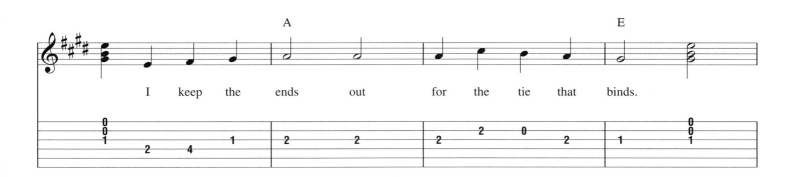

I keep the ends out for the tie that binds.

To Coda 2 ⊕

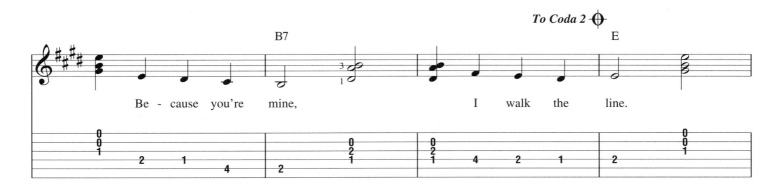

Be - cause you're mine, I walk the line.

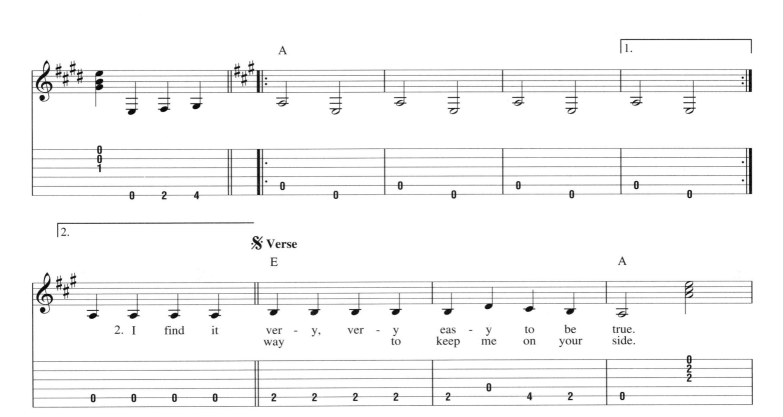

2. I find it ver - y, ver - y eas - y to be true.
way to keep me on your side.

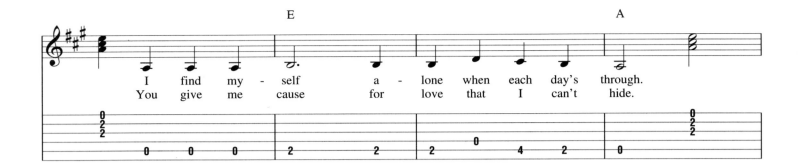

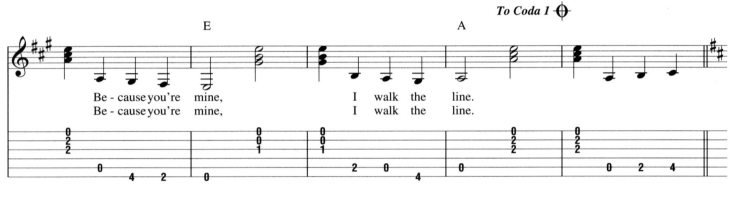

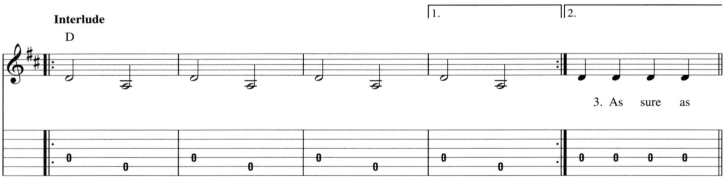

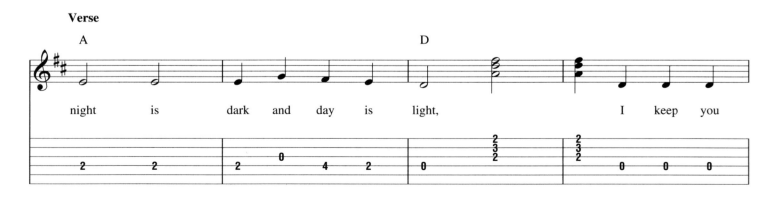

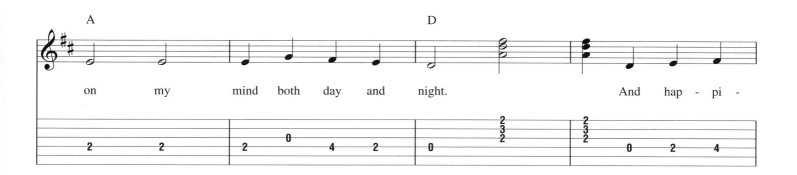

on my   mind both day and night.   And   hap - pi -

ness   I've   known proves that   it's   right.   Be - cause you're

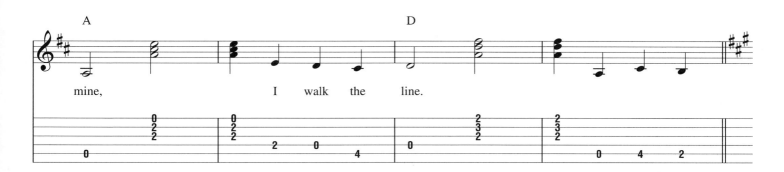

mine,   I   walk   the   line.

D.S. al Coda 1

Interlude

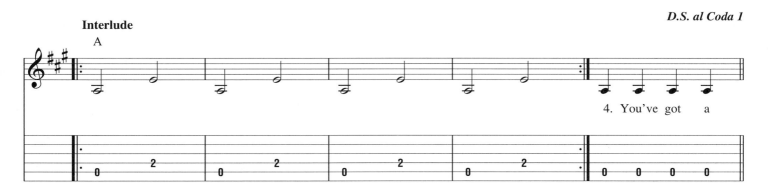

4. You've got   a

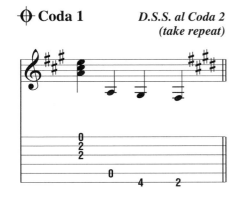

✛ **Coda 1**   *D.S.S. al Coda 2*   ✛ **Coda 2**
               (take repeat)

Repeat and fade

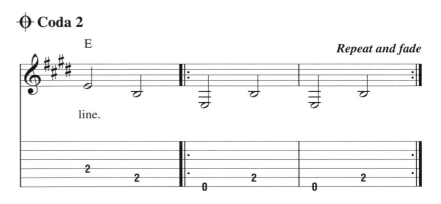

line.

I've Been Everywhere

Words and Music by Geoff Mack

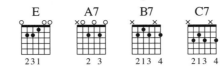

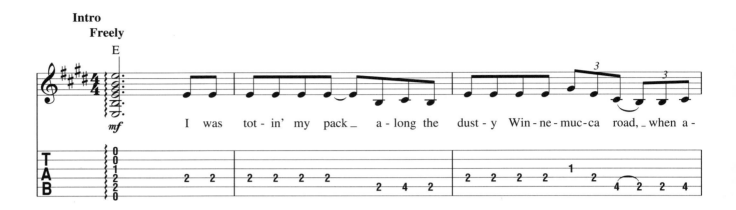

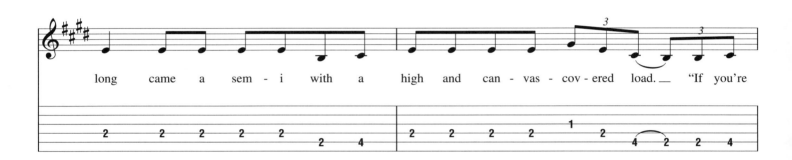

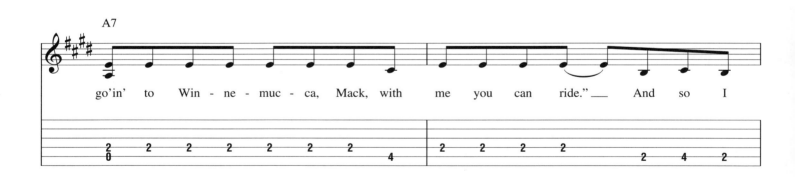

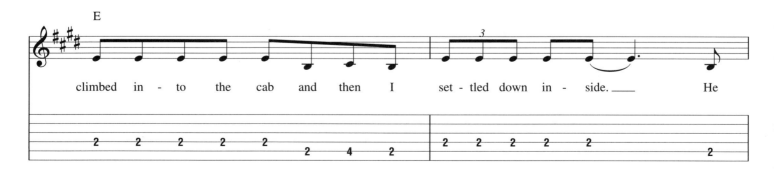

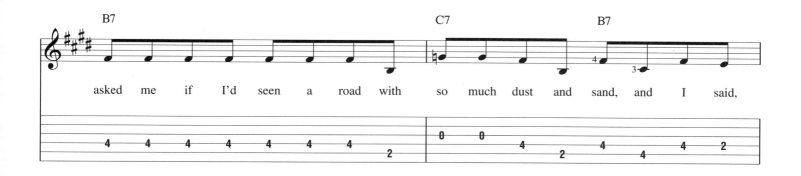

asked me if I'd seen a road with so much dust and sand, and I said,

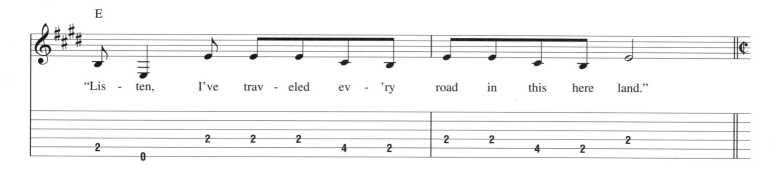

"Lis - ten, I've trav - eled ev - 'ry road in this here land."

Strum Pattern: 3, 6
Pick Pattern: 3

𝄋 **Chorus**
Moderately, in 2

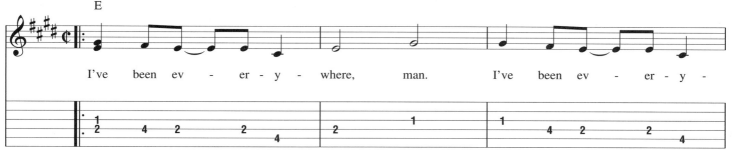

I've been ev – er – y – where, man. I've been ev – er – y –

where, man. 'Cross the des – erts, bare, man. I've

breathed the moun – tain air, man. Of trav - el I've had my

share, man. I've been ev - er - y - where.

Verse

1. I've been to Re - no, Chi - ca - go, Far - go, Min - ne - so - ta,
2.- 4. *See additional lyrics*

Buf - fa - lo, To - ron - to, Win - slow, Sa - ra - so - ta, Wich - i - ta, Tul - sa, Ot -

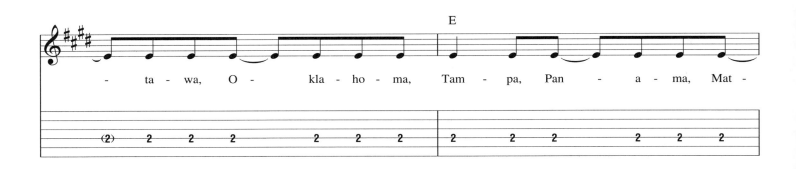

- ta - wa, O - kla - ho - ma, Tam - pa, Pan - a - ma, Mat -

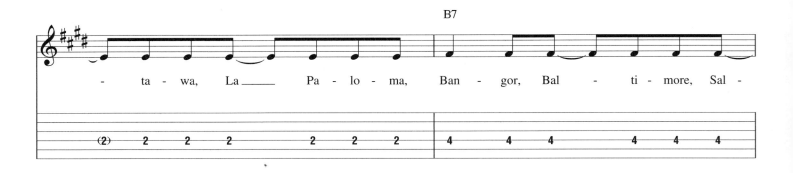

- ta - wa, La ___ Pa - lo - ma, Ban - gor, Bal - ti - more, Sal -

-va - dor, Am - a - ril - lo, To - co - pil - la, Bar - ran - quil - la,

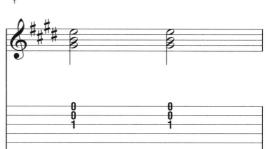

4th time, D.S. al Coda

Play 4 times

🪕 **Coda**

and Pa - dil - la, I'm a kil - ler.

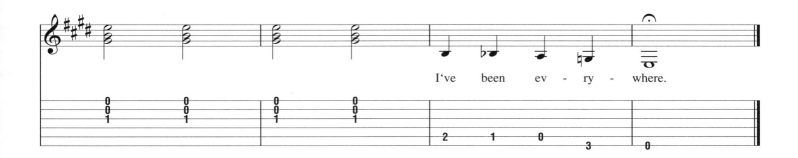

I've been ev - ry - where.

Additional Lyrics

2. I've been to Boston, Charleston, Dayton, Louisana,
   Washington, Houston, Kingston, Texarkana,
   Monterey, Ferriday, Santa Fe, Tallapoosa,
   Glen Rock, Black Rock, Little Rock, Oskaloosa,
   Tennessee, Hennessey, Chicopee, Spirit Lake,
   Grand Lake, Devil's Lake, Crater Lake for Pete's sake.

3. I've been to Louisville, Nashville, Knoxville, Ombabika,
   Shefferville, Jaclsonville, Waterville, Costa Rica,
   Pittsfield, Springfield, Bakersfield, Shreveport,
   Hackensack, Cadillac, Fond du Lac, Davenport,
   Idaho, Jellicoe, Argentina, Diamontina,
   Pasadena, Catalina, see what I mean a?

4. I've been to Pittsburgh, Parkersburg, Gravelburg, Colorado,
   Ellenburg, Rexburg, Vicksburg, El Dorado,
   Larrimore, Atmore, Haverstraw, Chattanika,
   Chaska, Nebraska, Alaska, Opelika,
   Baraboo, Waterloo, Kalamazoo, Kansas City,
   Sioux City, Cedar City, Dodge City, what a pity.

If I Were a Carpenter

Words and Music by Tim Hardin

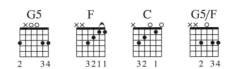

*Capo II

Strum Pattern: 3
Pick Pattern: 3

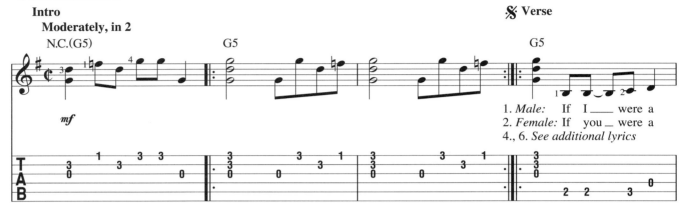

*Optional: To match recording, place capo at 2nd fret.

1. *Male:* If I ___ were a
2. *Female:* If you _ were a
4., 6. *See additional lyrics*

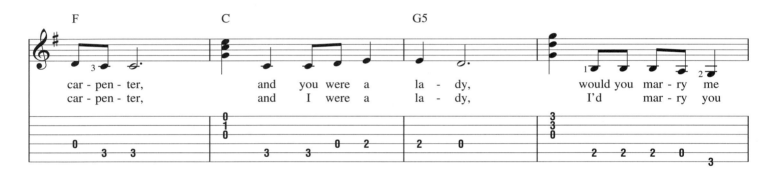

car - pen - ter,   and you were a la - dy,   would you mar - ry me
car - pen - ter,   and I were a la - dy,   I'd mar - ry you

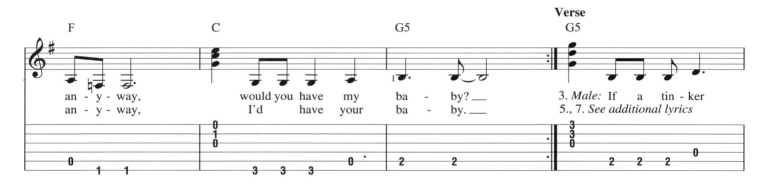

an - y - way,   would you have my ba - by? ___
an - y - way,   I'd have your ba - by. ___

3. *Male:* If a tin - ker
5., 7. *See additional lyrics*

was my trade, _   would I ___ still find you?   *Female:* I'd be car - ry - in' the

Additional Lyrics

4. *Male:*   If I were a miller and a mill wheel grindin',
             Would you miss your colored blouse and your soft shoes shinin'?

5. *Female:*   If you were a miller and mill wheel grindin',
             I'd not miss my colored blouse and my soft shoes shinin'.

6. *Male:*   If I worked my hands in wood, would you still love me?
   Female: I'd answer you, "Yes, I would. *Male:* And would you not be above me...

7.   ...If I were a carpenter, and you were a lady?
   Female: I'd marry you anyway, I'd have your baby.

Jackson

Words and Music by Billy Edd Wheeler and Jerry Leiber

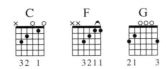

Strum Pattern: 3, 4
Pick Pattern: 3, 4

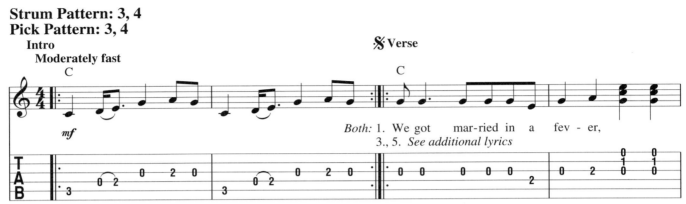

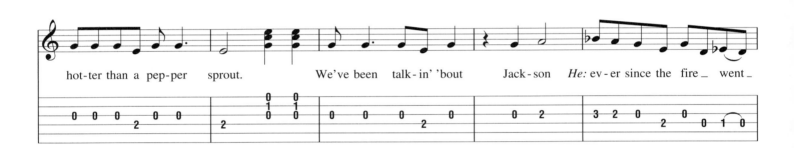

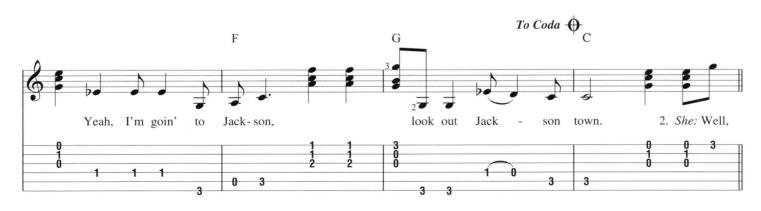

Additional Lyrics

3. *He:* When I breeze into that city,
     People gonna stoop and bow. *She:* Ha!
    He: All them women gonna make me
     Teach 'em what they don't know how.
     I'm goin' to Jackson.
     You turn loose a my coat,
     'Cause I'm goin' to Jackson.
    She: "Goodbye," that's all she wrote.

4. *She:* But they'll laugh at you in Jackson,
     And I'll be dancin' on a pony keg.
     They'll lead you 'round town like a scolded hound
     With your tail tucked between your legs.
     Yeah, go to Jackson
     You big-talkin' man,
     And I'll be waitin' in Jackson,
     Behind my Japan fan.

5. *Both:* Well, now, we got married in a fever,
     Hotter than a pepper sprout.
     We've been talkin' 'bout Jackson
     Ever since the fire went out.
     I'm goin' to Jackson,
     And that's a fact.
     Yeah, we're goin' to Jackson,
     Ain't never comin' back.

Katy Too

Words and Music by John R. Cash and Jack Clement

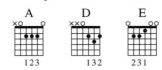

*Capo I

Strum Pattern: 3
Pick Pattern: 3

Intro
Moderately, in 2

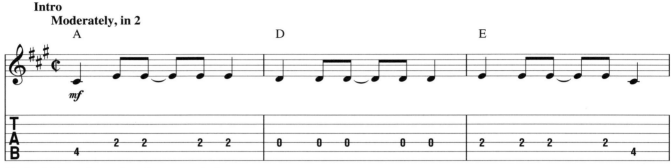

*Optional: To match recording, place capo at 1st fret.

℅ Verse

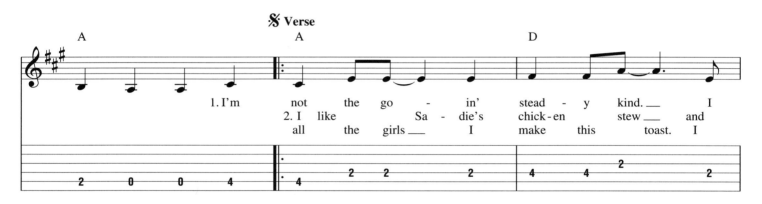

1. I'm not the go - in' stead - y kind. ___ I
2. I like Sa - die's chick - en stew ___ and
   all the girls ___ I make this toast. I

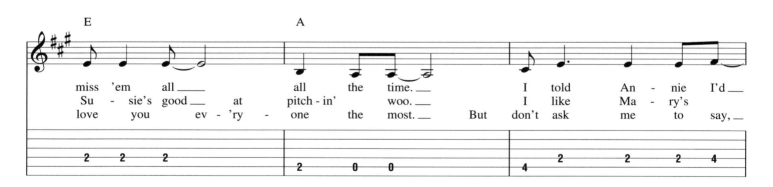

miss 'em all ___ all the time. ___ I told An - nie I'd ___
Su - sie's good ___ at pitch - in' woo. ___ I like Ma - ry's
love you ev - 'ry - one the most. ___ But don't ask me to say,

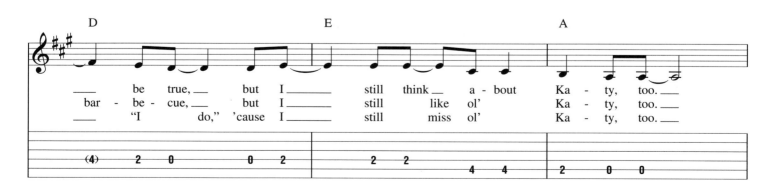

___ be true, ___ but I still think ___ a - bout Ka - ty, too. ___
bar - be - cue, ___ but I still like ol' Ka - ty, too. ___
___ "I do," 'cause I still miss ol' Ka - ty, too. ___

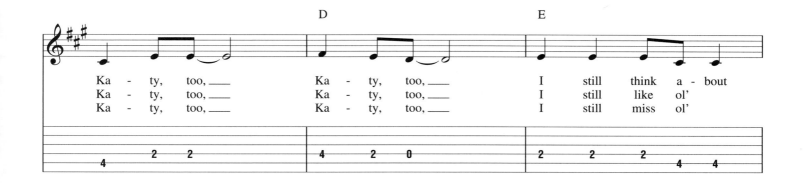

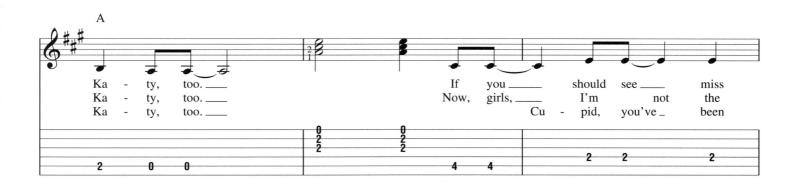

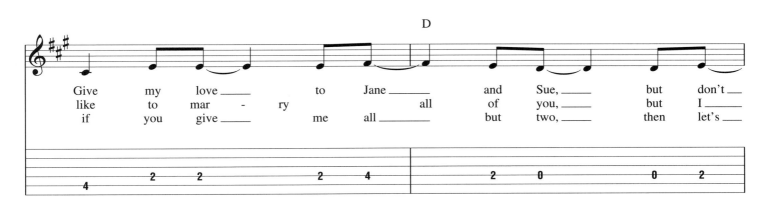

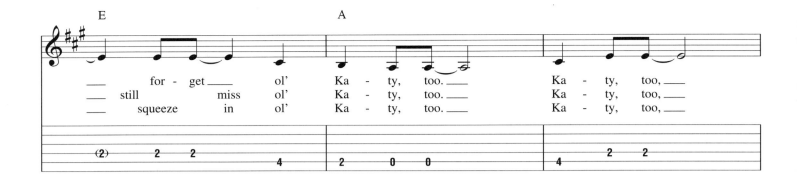

___ for - get ___ ol' Ka - ty, too. ___ Ka - ty, too, ___
___ still miss ol' Ka - ty, too. ___ Ka - ty, too, ___
___ squeeze in ol' Ka - ty, too. ___ Ka - ty, too, ___

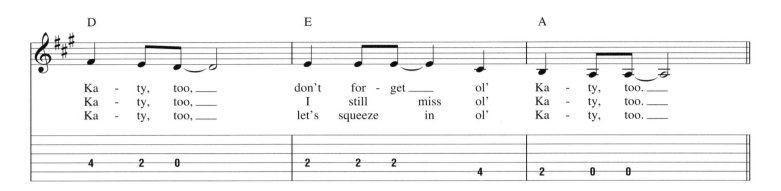

Ka - ty, too, ___ don't for - get ___ ol' Ka - ty, too. ___
Ka - ty, too, ___ I still miss ol' Ka - ty, too. ___
Ka - ty, too, ___ let's squeeze in ol' Ka - ty, too. ___

Interlude

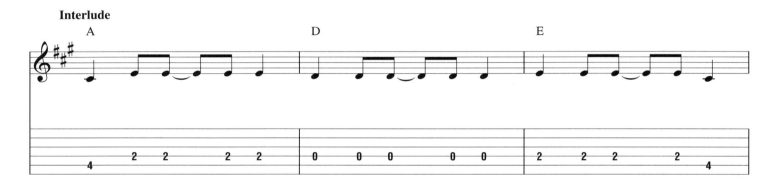

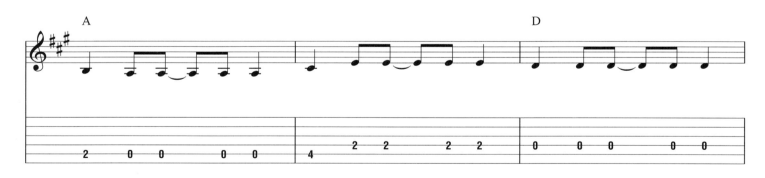

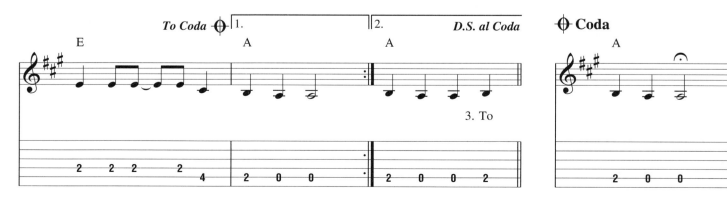

48

(Ghost) Riders in the Sky
(A Cowboy Legend)

By Stan Jones

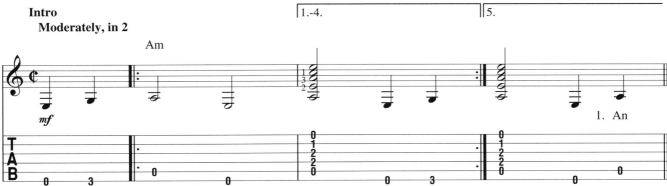

*Capo I

Strum Pattern: 1, 3
Pick Pattern: 1, 3

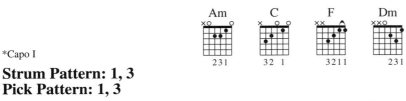

*Optional: To match recording, place capo at 1st fret.

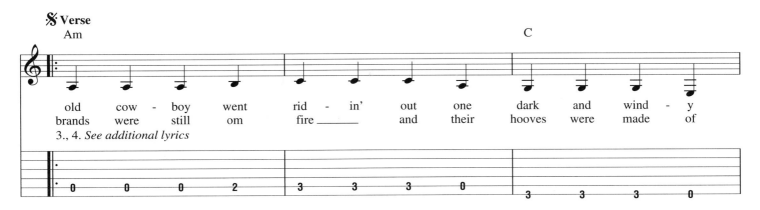

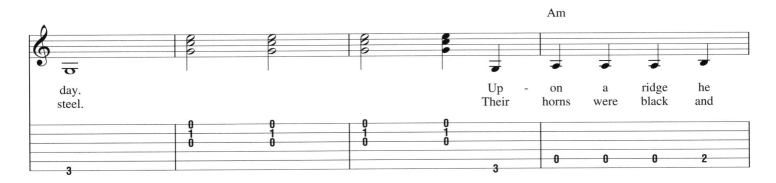

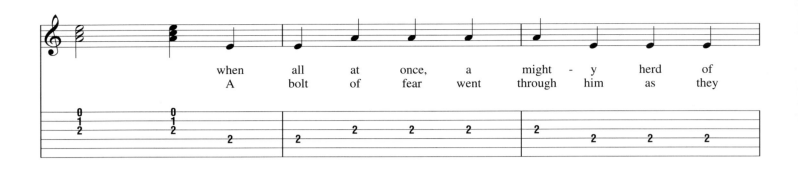

when all at once, a might - y herd of
A bolt of fear once, went through him as of they

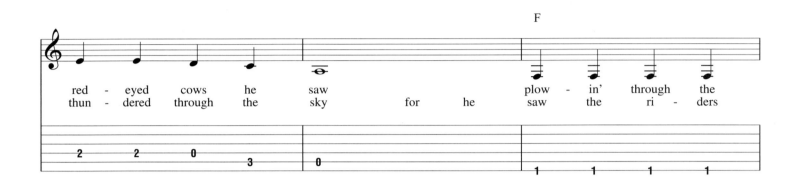

F

red - eyed cows he saw plow - in' through the
thun - dered through the sky for he saw the ri - ders

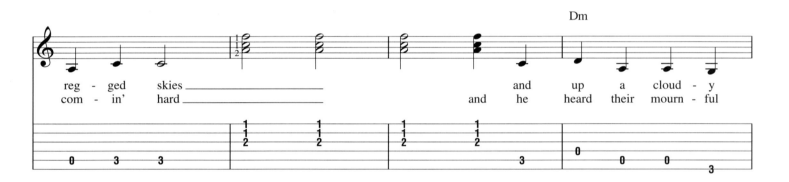

Dm

reg - ged skies _____ and up a cloud - y
com - in' hard _____ and he heard their mourn - ful

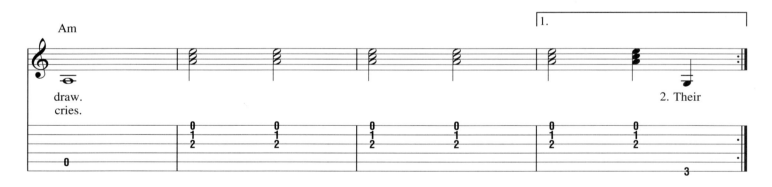

Am

1.

draw.
cries.

2. Their

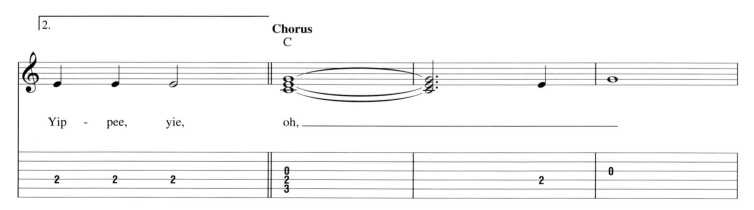

2.

Chorus
C

Yip - pee, yie, oh, _____

50

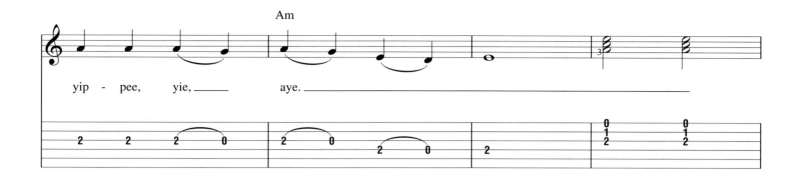

yip - pee, yie, _____ aye. _____

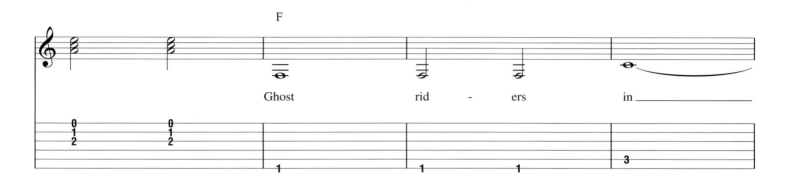

Ghost   rid - ers   in _____

To Coda ⊕

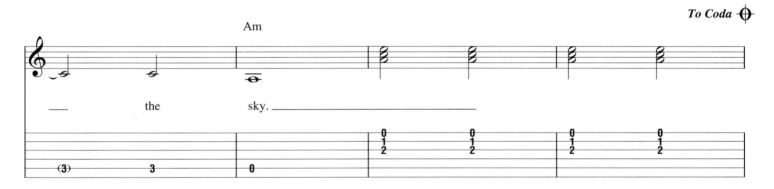

_____   the   sky. _____

Interlude

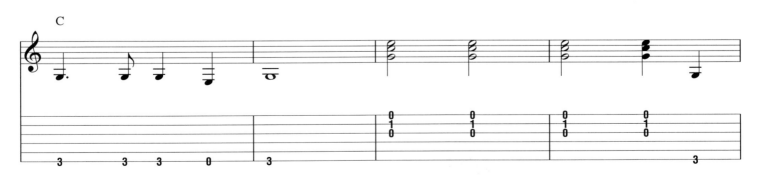

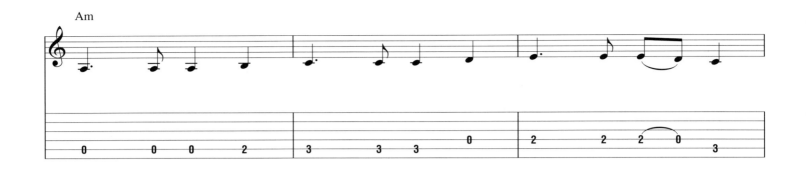

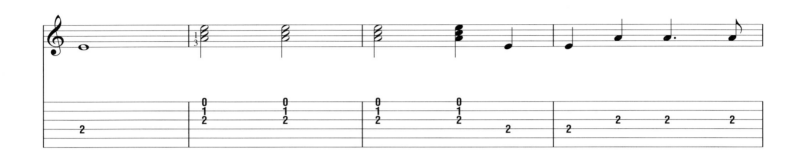

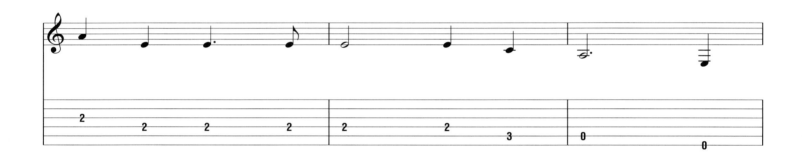

D.S. al Coda
(take repeat)

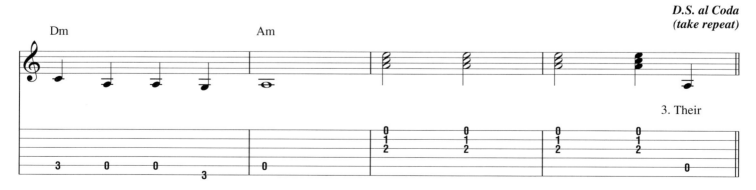

3. Their

⊕ Coda

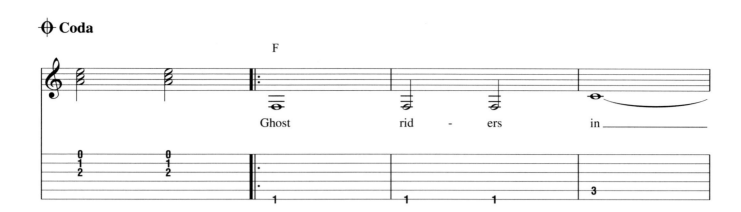

Ghost rid - ers in ___

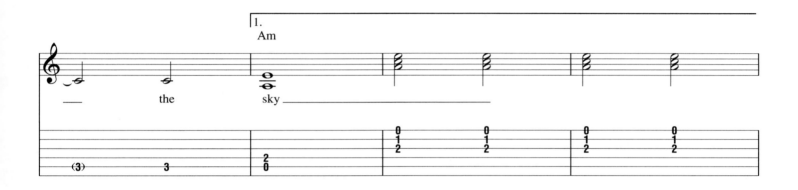

___ the sky ___

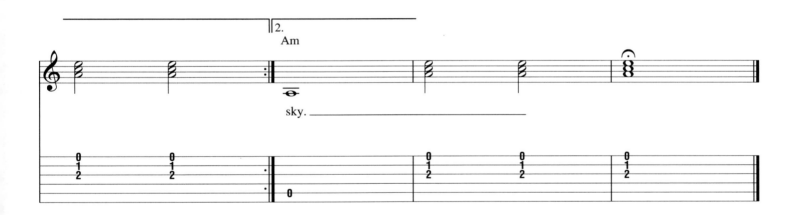

sky. ___

Additional Lyrics

3. Their faces gaunt, their eyes are blurred, their shirts all soaked with sweat.
   He's ridin' hard to carch that herd, but ain't caught 'em yet
   'Cause they've got to ride forever on that range up in the sky
   On horses snortin' fire. As they ride on, hear their cry.

4. As the riders loped on by him, he heard one call his name,
   "If you want to save your soul from Hell a ridin' on our range,
   Then, cowboy, change your ways today, or with us you will ride,
   Tryin' to catch the Devil's herd across these endless skies."

Luther's Boogie
(Luther Played the Boogie)

Words and Music by John R. Cash

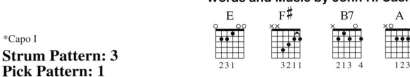

*Capo I

Strum Pattern: 3
Pick Pattern: 1

Intro
Moderately, in 2

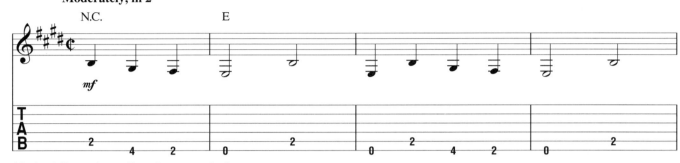

*Optional: To match recording, place capo at 1st fret.

Verse

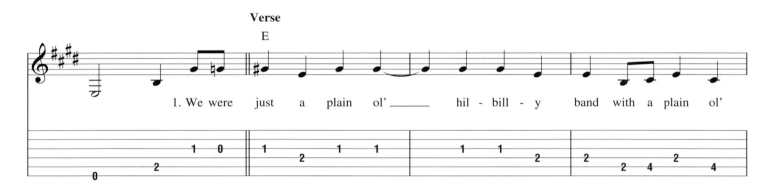

1. We were just a plain ol' _____ hil - bill - y band with a plain ol' coun - try style. We nev - er played the kind of

songs that would drive an - y - bod - y wild. _____ We played a

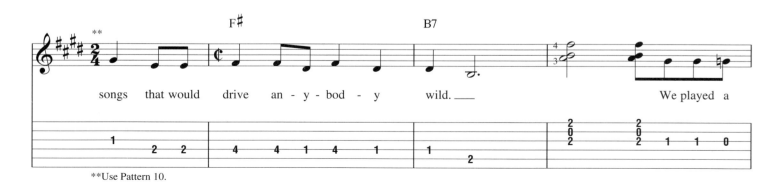

**Use Pattern 10.

𝄋 Chorus

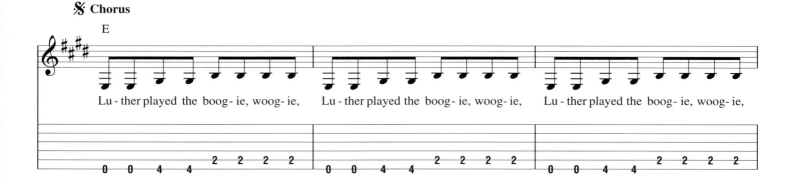

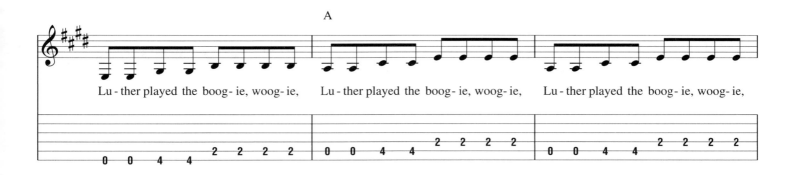

Interlude

kind of ____ way.

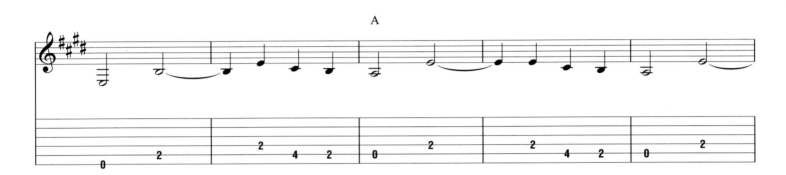

To Coda

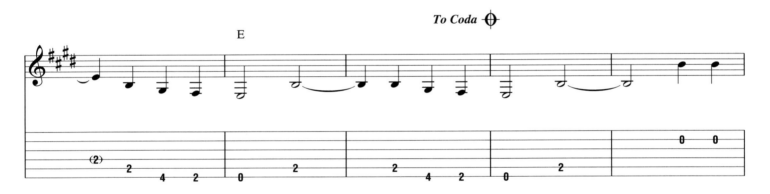

Verse

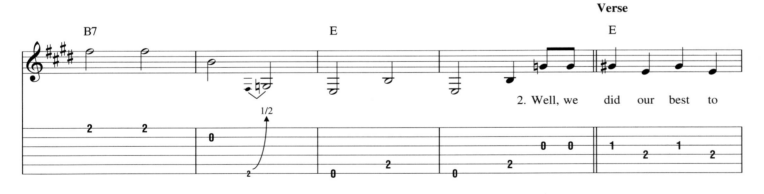

2. Well, we did our best to

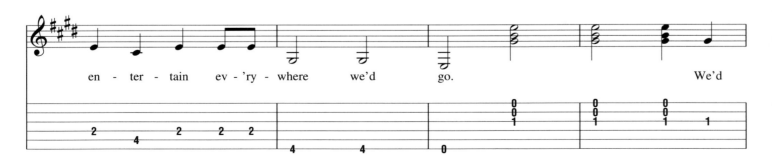

en - ter - tain ev - 'ry - where we'd go. We'd

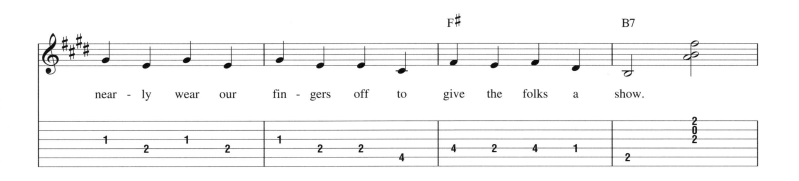

near - ly wear our fin - gers off to give the folks a show.

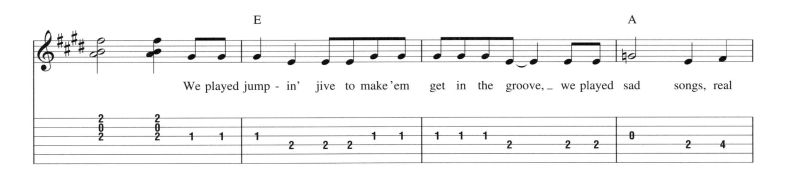

We played jump - in' jive to make 'em get in the groove, __ we played sad songs, real

slow and sweet, but the on - ly thing that - 'd make 'em move was, oo,

D.S. al Coda 🎵 **Coda** **Free time**

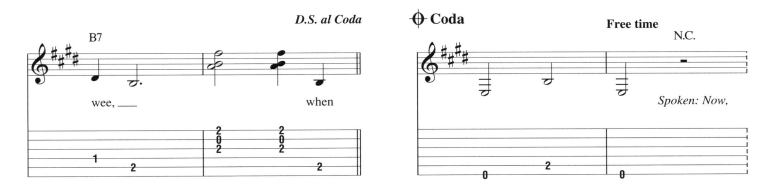

wee, __ when

Spoken: Now,

A tempo

didn't Luther play the boogie strange?

The Man in Black

Words and Music by John R. Cash

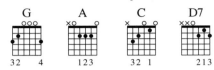

*Capo III

Strum Pattern: 4
Pick Pattern: 6

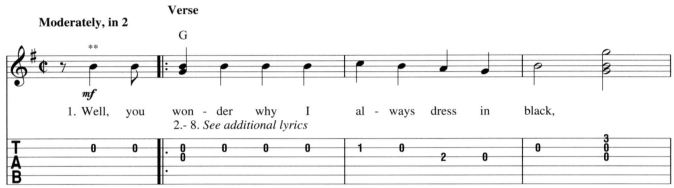

*Optional: To match recording, place capo at 3rd fret.
**Sung one octave lower.

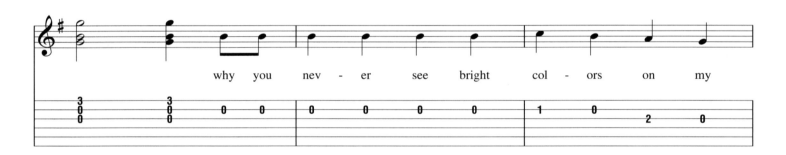

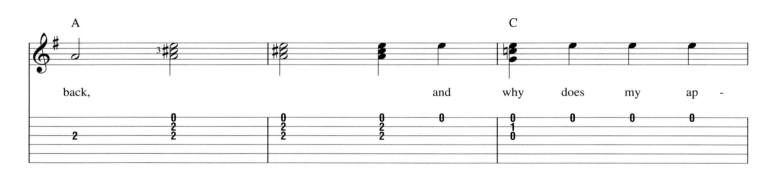

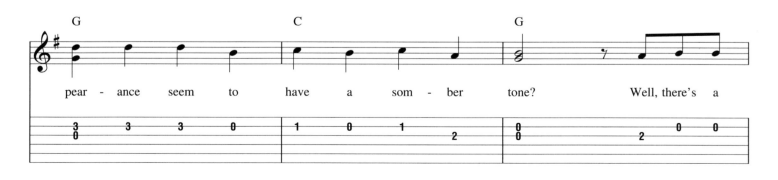

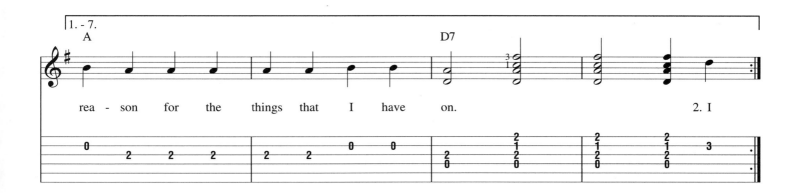

rea - son for the things that I have on. 2. I

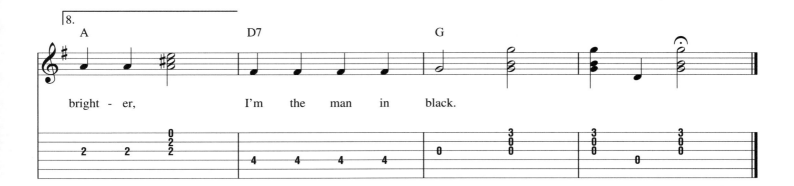

bright - er, I'm the man in black.

Additional Lyrics

2. I wear the black for the poor and the beaten down
   Livin' in the hopeless, hungry side of town.
   I wear it for the prisoner who has long paid for his crime
   That is there because he's a victim of the times.

3. I wear the black for those who've never read
   Or listened to the words that Jesus said
   About the road to happiness through love and charity.
   Why, you'd think he's talkin' straight to you and me.

4. Well, we're doin' mighty fine, I do suppose
   In our streak-o'-lightnin' cars and fancy clothes.
   But just so we're reminded of the ones who are held back,
   Up front there ought to be a man in black.

5. I wear it for the sick and lonely old,
   For the reckless ones whose bad trip left them cold.
   I wear the black in mournin' for the lives that could have been;
   Each week we lose a hundred fine young men.

6. And I wear it for the thousands who have died
   Believin' that the Lord was on their side.
   I wear it for another hundred thousand who have died.
   Believin' that we all were on their side.

7. Well, there's things that never will be right, I know,
   And things need changin' ev'rywhere you go.
   But till we start to make a move to make a few things right,
   You'll never see me wear a suit of white.

8. Oh, I'd love to wear a rainbow ev'ry day.
   And tell the world that ev'rything's okay.
   But I'll try to carry off a little darkness on my back;
   Till things are brighter, I'm the man in black.

One Piece at a Time

Words and Music by Wayne Kemp

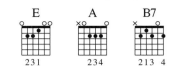

*Capo 1

Strum Pattern: 3
Pick Pattern: 3

Intro
Moderately, in 2

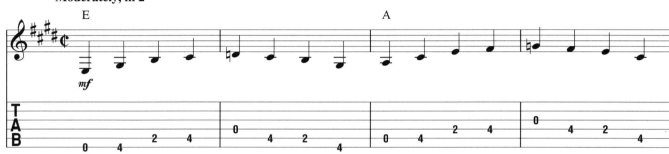

*Optional: To match recording, place capo at 1st fret.

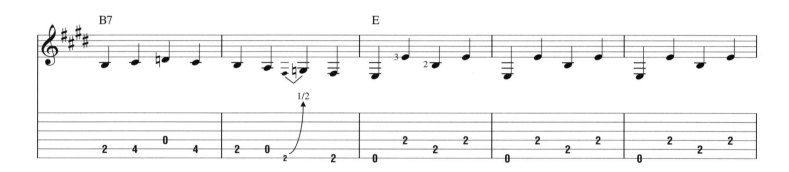

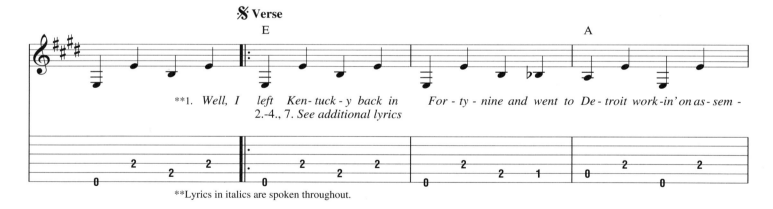

**1. Well, I left Ken-tuck-y back in For-ty-nine and went to De-troit work-in' on as-sem-
2.-4., 7. See additional lyrics

**Lyrics in italics are spoken throughout.

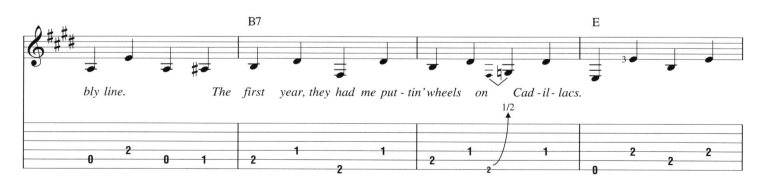

bly line.   The first year, they had me put-tin' wheels on Cad-il-lacs.

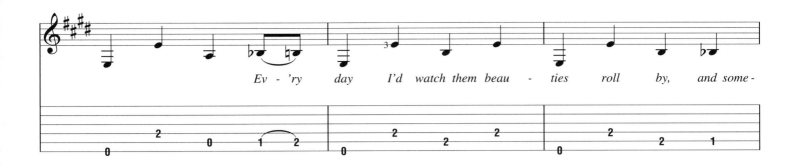

Ev - 'ry day I'd watch them beau - ties roll by, and some -

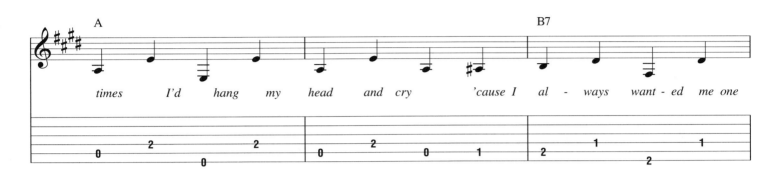

times I'd hang my head and cry 'cause I al - ways want - ed me one

4th time, To Coda 1 🔶 | 1. | 2.

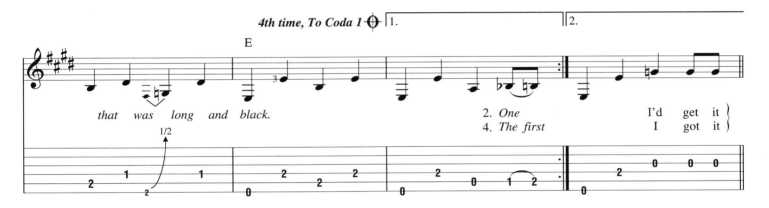

that was long and black.

2. One ... I'd get it ⎫
4. *The first* ... I got it ⎭

Chorus

one piece at a time, ___ and it ⎰ would - n't ⎱ cost me a dime. ___
⎱ did - n't ⎰

___ You'll know it's me ___ when I ___ come through your

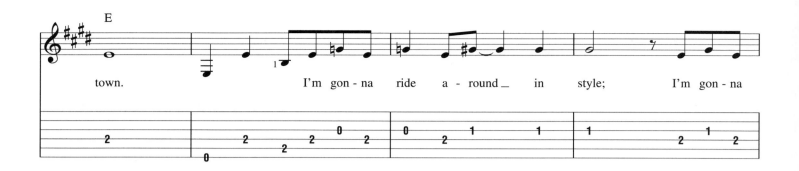

town.   I'm gon - na ride a - round __ in style;   I'm gon - na

drive ev - 'ry - bod - y wild _____ 'cause I'll have the on - ly

To Coda 2 ⊕   *D.S. al Coda 1*   ⊕ **Coda 1**
(take repeat)

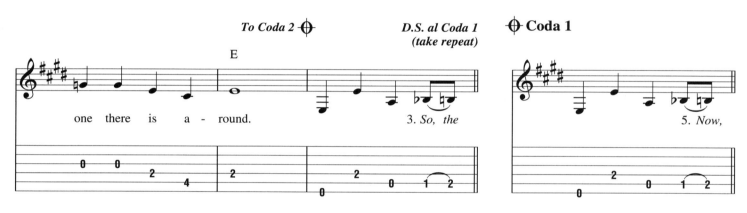

one there is a - round.   *3. So, the*   *5. Now,*

Verse

up   to   now,   my plan   went all right,   'til we tried to put it all   to - geth -
6. See additional lyrics

er one night,   and that's when we no - ticed that some - thing was def - i - nite - ly

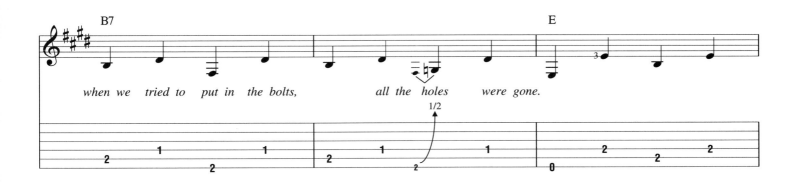

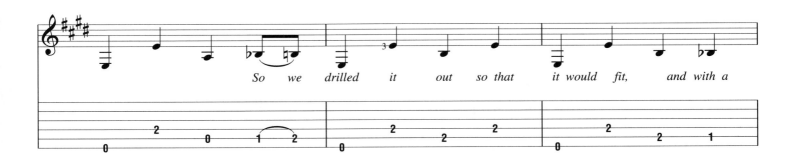

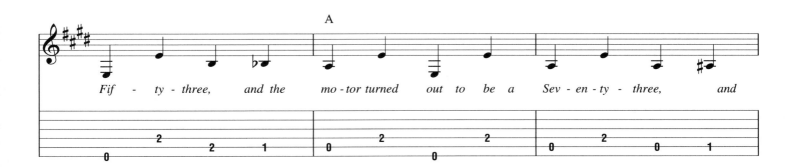

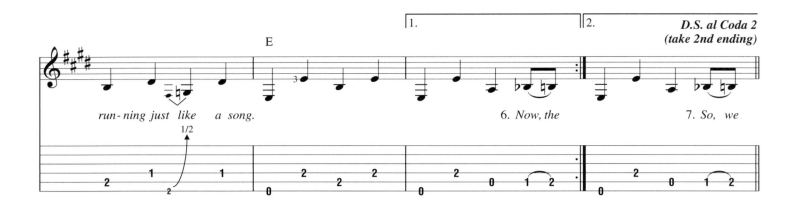

D.S. al Coda 2
(take 2nd ending)

run - ning just like a song.

6. Now, the

7. So, we

Coda 2

Interlude

1.-9.

See additional lyrics

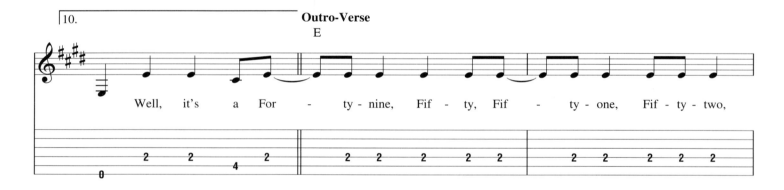

10.

Outro-Verse

Well, it's a For - ty - nine, Fif - ty, Fif - ty - one, Fif - ty - two,

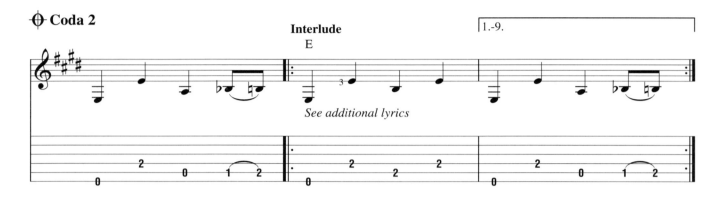

Fif - ty - three, Fif - ty - four, Fif - ty - five, Fif - ty - six, Fif - ty - sev - en, Fif - ty - eight,

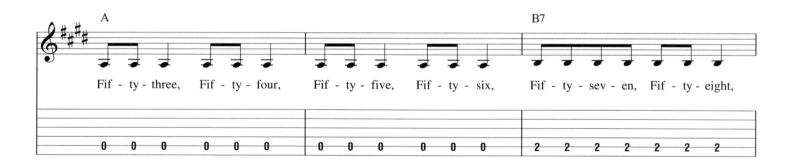

Fif - ty - nine au - to - mo - bile. ____ It's a Six - ty, six - ty - one,

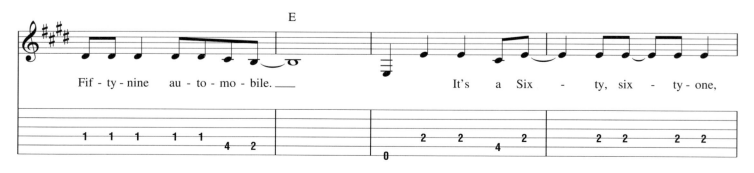

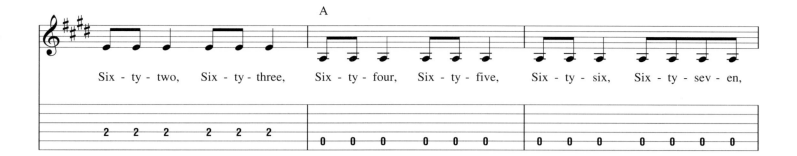

Six - ty - two, Six - ty - three, Six - ty - four, Six - ty - five, Six - ty - six, Six - ty - sev - en,

Six - ty - eight, Six - ty - nine, Sev - en - ty au - to - mo - bile.

Additional Lyrics

2. *One day I devised myself a plan*
   That should be envy of most any man.
   I'd sneak it out of there in a lunch box in my hand.
   Now, gettin' caught meant gettin' fired,
   But I figured I'd have it all by the time I retired.
   I'd have me a car worth at least a hundred grand.

3. *So, the very next day when I punched in*
   With my big lunch box and with help from my friend,
   I left that day with a lunch box full of gears.
   I've never considered myself a thief,
   But GM wouldn't miss just one little piece,
   Especially if I strung it out over several years.

4. *The first day, I got me a fuel pump,*
   And the next day I got me an engine and a trunk.
   Then I got me a transmission and all the chrome.
   The little things I could get in my big lunch box
   Like nuts and bolts and all four shocks.
   But the big stuff we snuck out in my buddy's mobile home.

6. *Now, the headlights, they was another sight,*
   We had two on the left and one on the right.
   But when we pulled out the switch, all three of 'em come on.
   The back end looked kinda funny, too.
   But we put it together, and when we got through,
   Well, that's when we noticed that we only had one tail fin.
   About that time, my wife walked out,
   And I could see in her eyes that she had her doubts.
   But she opened the door and said, "Honey, take me for a spin."

7. *So, we drove uptown just to get the tags,*
   And I headed her right on down the main drag.
   I could hear everybody laughin' for blocks around.
   But, up there at the court house, they didn't laugh,
   'Cause to type it up, it took the whole staff.
   And when they got through, the title weighed sixty pounds.

Interlude Ah, yeah, Red Rider, this is the Cottonmouth
   In the Psychobilly Cadillac, come on. Hah.
   Ah, this is the Cottonmouth, and negatory
   On the cost of this mo-chine, there, Red Rider.
   You might say I went right up to the factory
   And picked it up; it's cheaper that way.
   Ah, what model is it?

Orange Blossom Special

Words and Music by Ervin T. Rouse

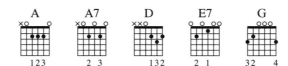

*Capo III
Strum Pattern: 3, 4
Pick Pattern: 3

Intro
Moderately, in 2

*Optional: To match recording, place capo at 3rd fret.
**Harmonica & gtr. arr. for gtr., next 9 meas.

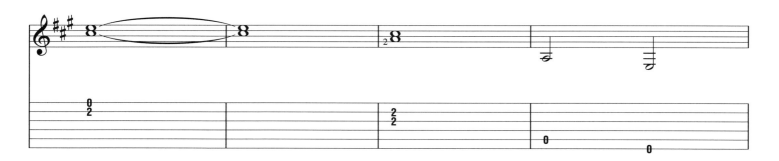

𝄋 Verse

2.Well, I'm go - in' down to Flor - 'da
talk a - bout a ram - blin',
Look yon - der com - in',
and
she's the

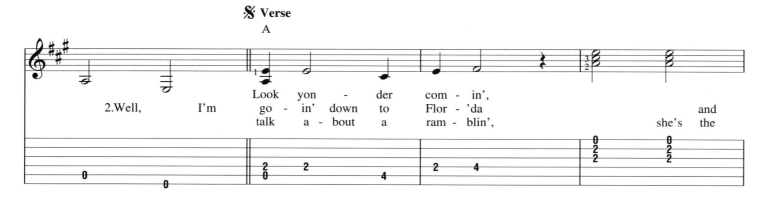

com - in' down that rail - road track. Hey,
get some sand in my shoes, or
fast - est train on the line.

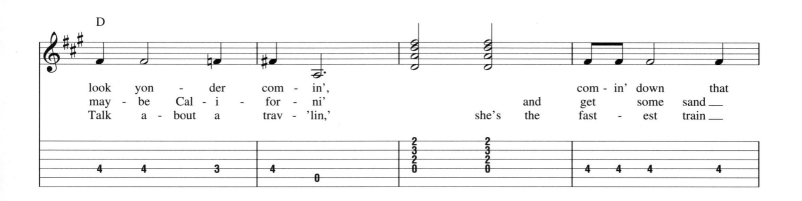

look yon - der com - in', com - in' down that
may - be Cal - i - for - ni' and get some sand ___
Talk a - bout a trav - 'lin,' she's the fast - est train ___

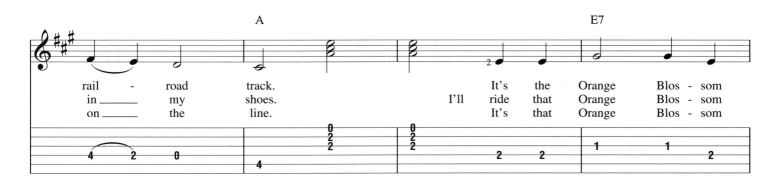

rail - road track. It's the Orange Blos - som
in ___ my shoes. I'll ride that Orange Blos - som
on ___ the line. It's that Orange Blos - som

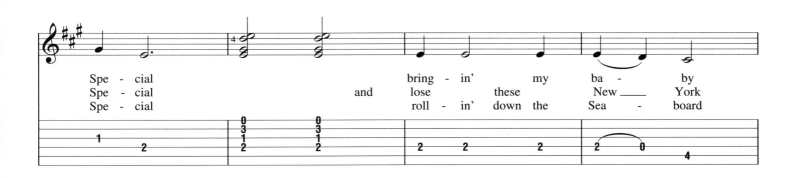

Spe - cial bring - in' my ba - by
Spe - cial and lose these New ___ York
Spe - cial roll - in' down the Sea - board

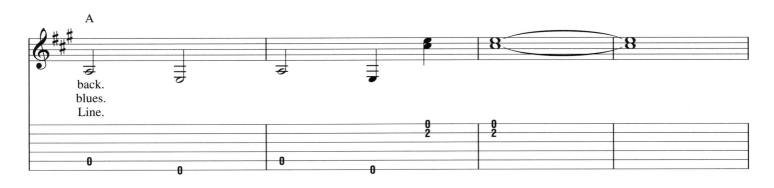

back.
blues.
Line.

3rd time, To Coda 2 ⊕

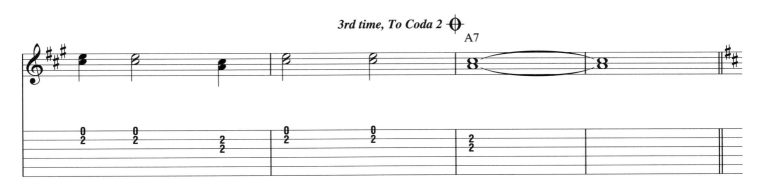

Interlude

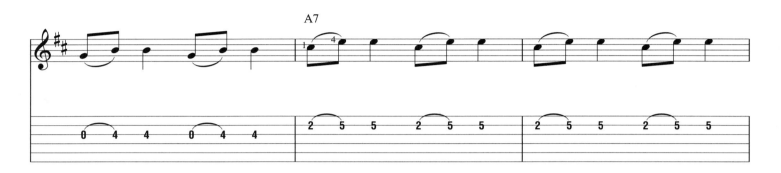

*Optional: Hammer on to 2nd string, 7th fret.

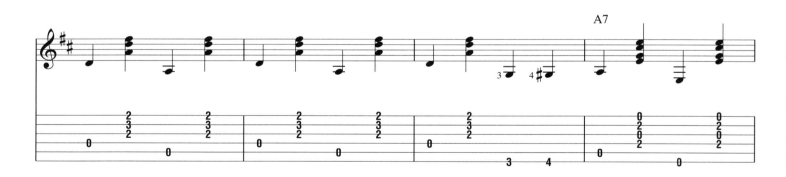

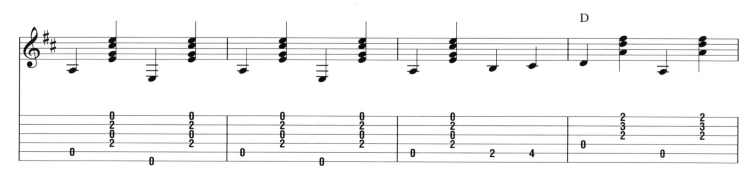

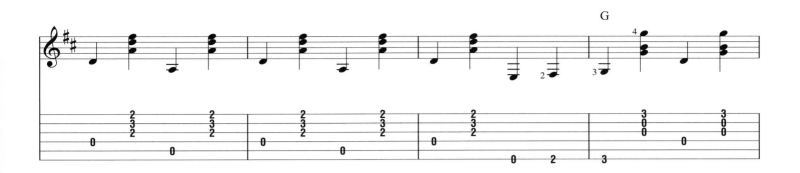

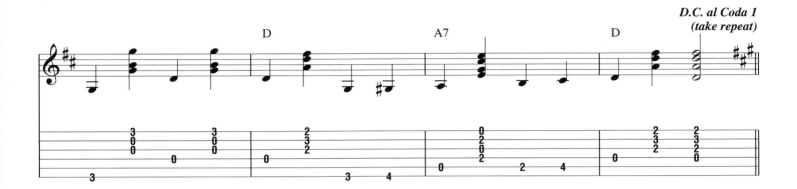

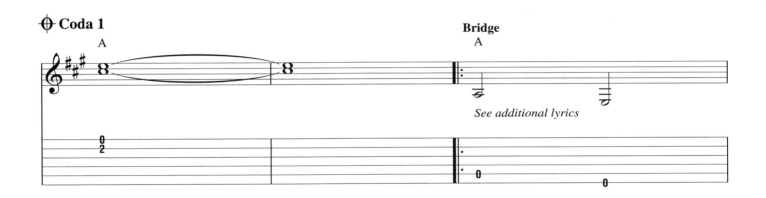

See additional lyrics

3. Hey,

Additional Lyrics

Bridge Spoken: (Say man, when you goin' back to Florida?)
When am I goin' back to Florida? I don't know. Don't reckon I ever will.
(Ain't you worried about gettin' your nourishment in New York?)
Uh, I don't care if I do, die, do, die, do, die, do, die, do, die.

Ring of Fire

Words and Music by Merle Kilgore and June Carter

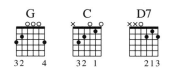

*Strum Pattern: 2
*Pick Pattern: 1

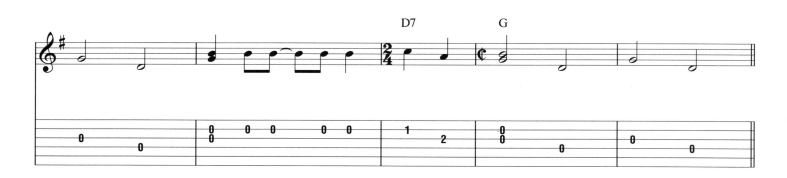

*Use Pattern 10 for $\frac{2}{4}$ meas.

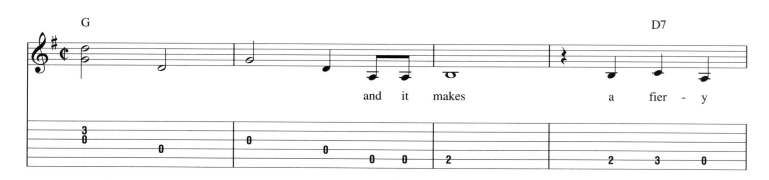

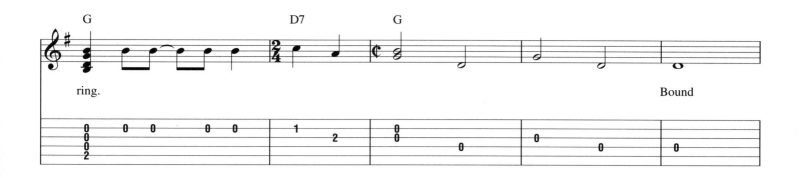

ring.   Bound

by   wild   de - sire,

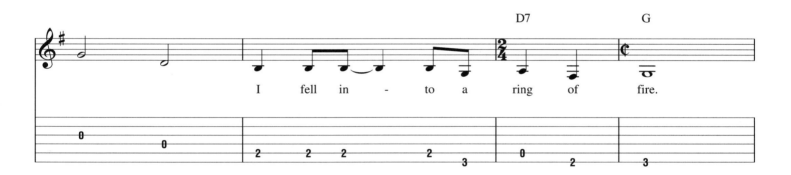

I   fell   in - to   a   ring   of   fire.

𝄋 Chorus

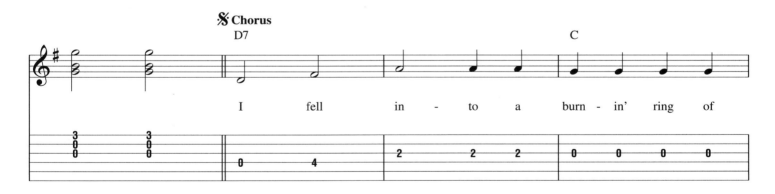

I   fell   in - to   a   burn - in'   ring   of

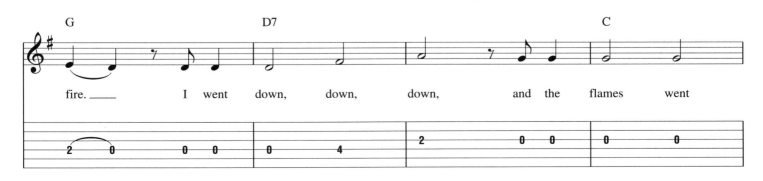

fire. _____   I   went   down,   down,   down,   and   the   flames   went

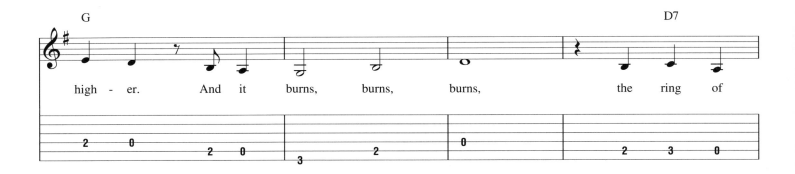

high - er. And it burns, burns, burns, the ring of

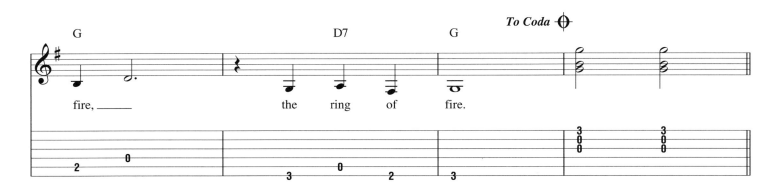

To Coda ⊕

fire, _____ the ring of fire.

Interlude

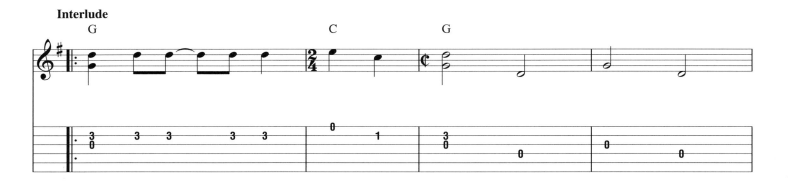

2nd time, D.S. al Coda

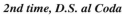

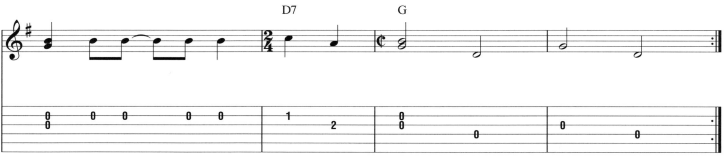

⊕ **Coda**

Verse

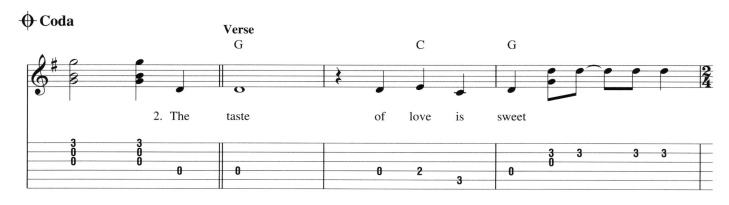

2. The taste of love is sweet

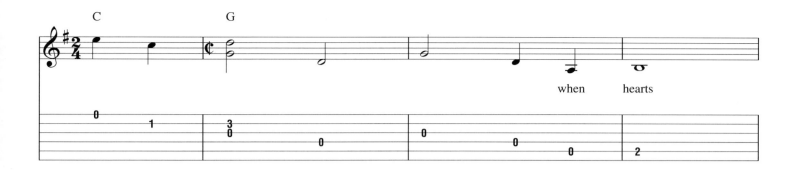

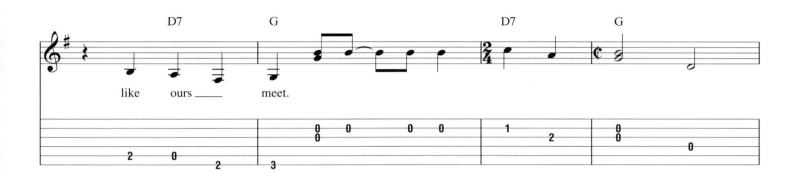

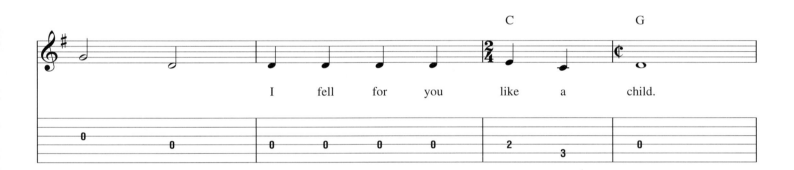

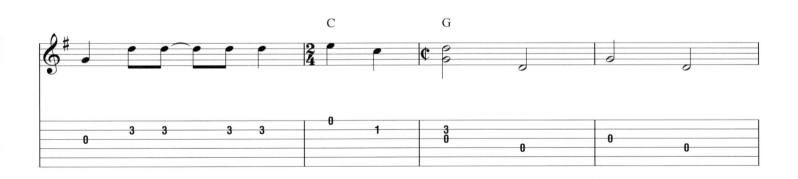

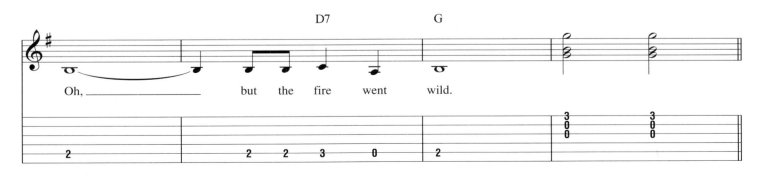

Chorus

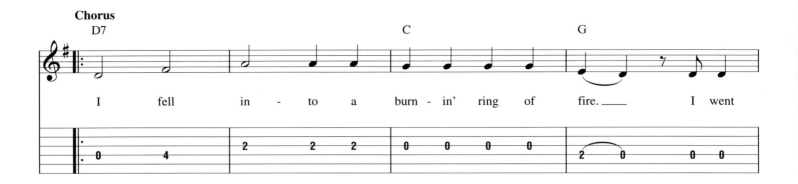

I fell in-to a burn-in' ring of fire. ___ I went

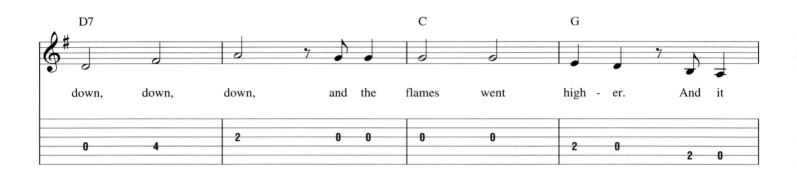

down, down, down, and the flames went high - er. And it

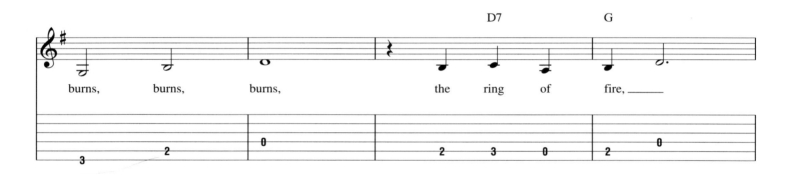

burns, burns, burns, the ring of fire, ___

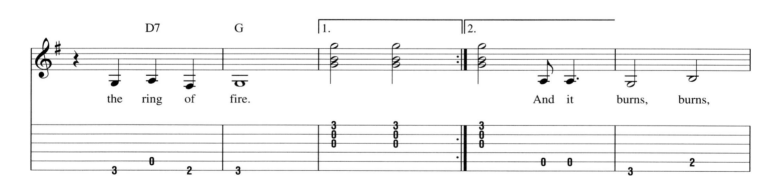

the ring of fire. And it burns, burns,

Repeat and fade

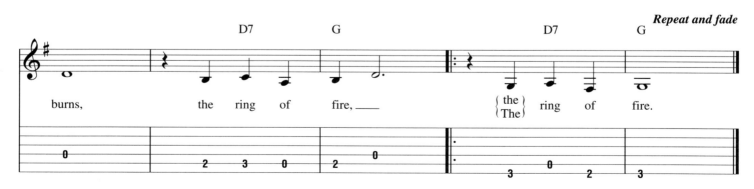

burns, the ring of fire, ___ { the / The } ring of fire.

Sunday Mornin' Comin' Down

Words and Music by Kris Kristofferson

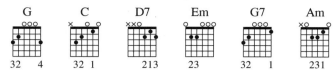

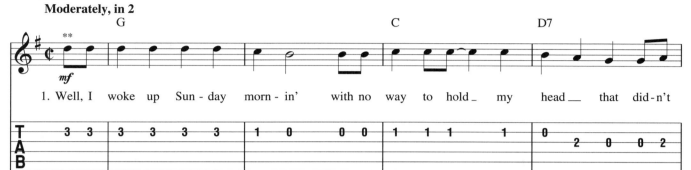

*Capo I

Strum Pattern: 3, 4
Pick Pattern: 3, 4

Verse
Moderately, in 2

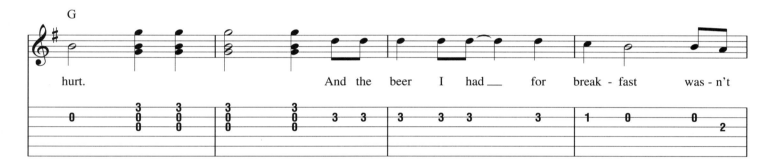

1. Well, I woke up Sun-day morn-in' with no way to hold my head that did-n't

*Optional: To match recording, place capo at 1st fret.

**Sung one octave lower.

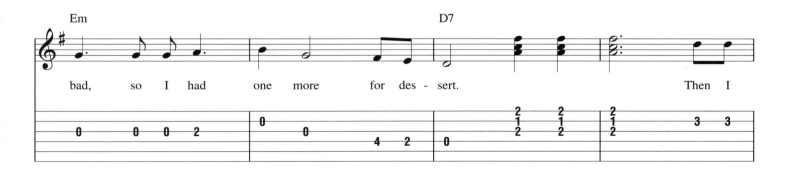

hurt. And the beer I had for break-fast was-n't

bad, so I had one more for des-sert. Then I

fum-bled in my clos-et, through my clothes and found my clean-est dir-ty

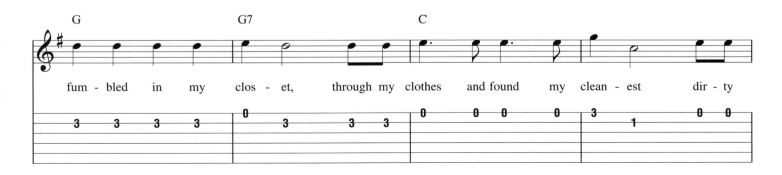

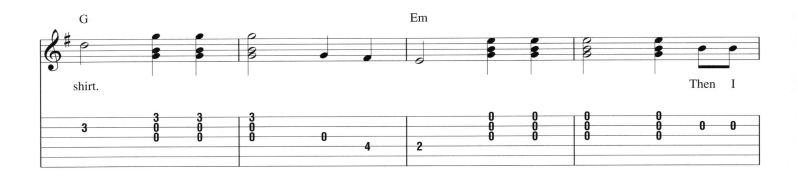

shirt.

Then I

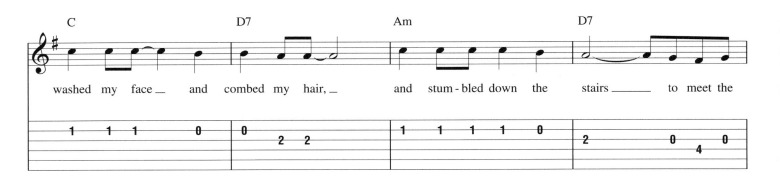

washed my face ___ and combed my hair, ___ and stum-bled down the stairs _____ to meet the

Verse

day.

2. I'd smoked my mind ___ the night be-fore ___
3. *See additional lyrics*

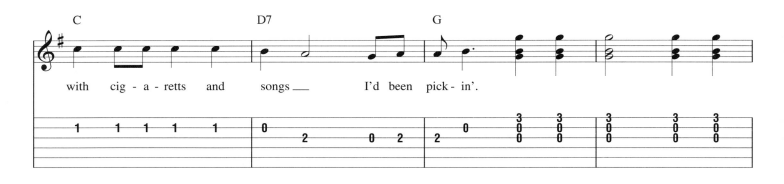

with cig-a-retts and songs ___ I'd been pick-in'.

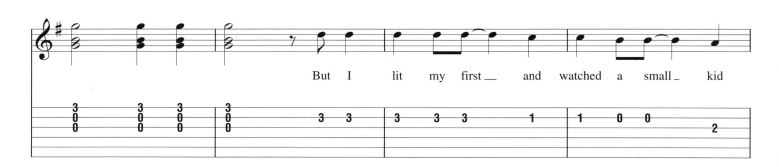

But I lit my first ___ and watched a small ___ kid

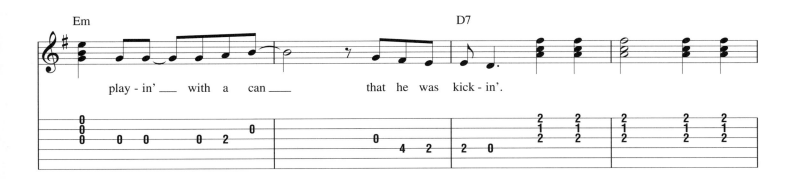

play - in' __ with a can __ that he was kick - in'.

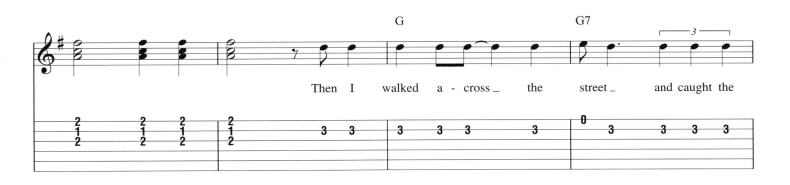

Then I walked a - cross __ the street __ and caught the

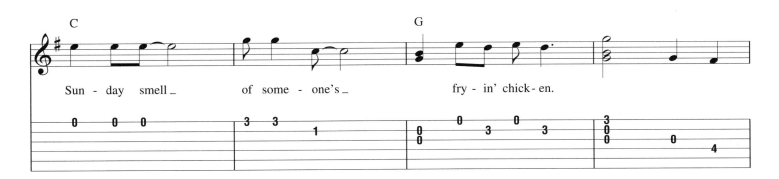

Sun - day smell __ of some - one's __ fry - in' chick - en.

And, Lord, it took me back __ to some - thin' that I

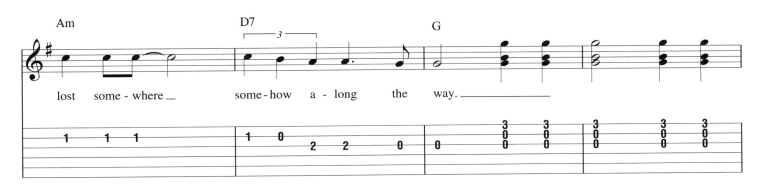

lost some - where __ some - how a - long the way. _____

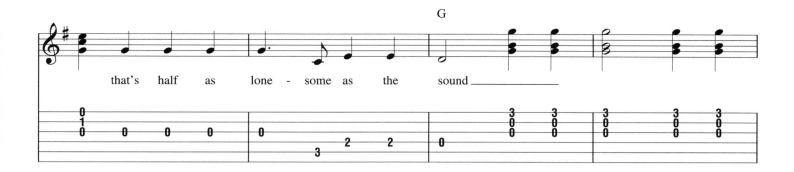

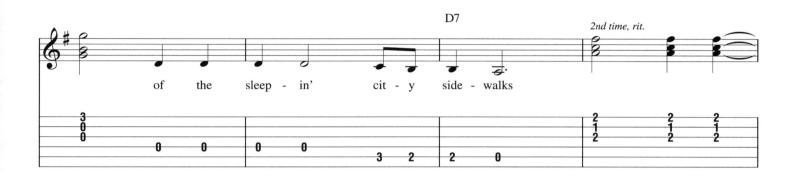

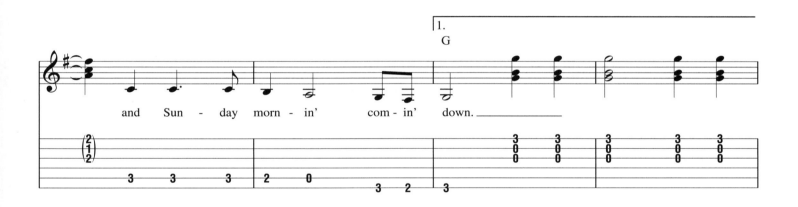

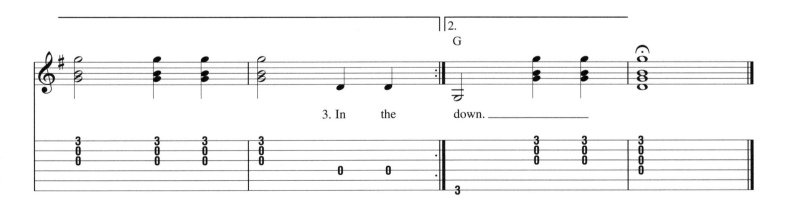

Additional Lyrics

3. In the park I saw a daddy with a laughin' little girl that he was swingin',
And I stopped beside a Sunday school and listened to the songs they were singin'
Then I headed down the streets, and somewhere far away a lonely bell was ringin',
And it echoed thru the canyons like the disappearing dreams of yesterday.

Tennessee Flat Top Box

Words and Music by Johnny R. Cash

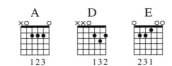

*Capo I

Strum Pattern: 3, 5
Pick Pattern: 1, 3

Intro
Moderately, in 2

*Optional: To match recording, place capo at 1st fret.

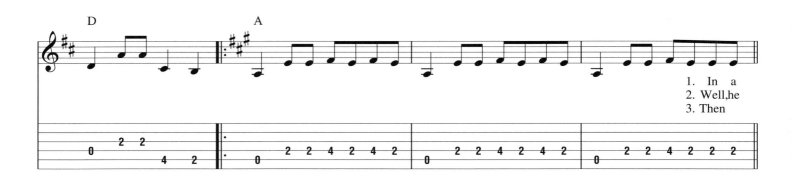

1. In a
2. Well, he
3. Then

lit - tle   cab - a - ret   in a   south   Tex - as
could - n't   ride   or   wran - gle,   and he   nev - er   cared to
one   day,   he   was   gone,   and   no   one   ev - er

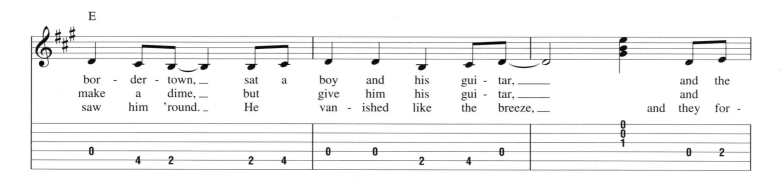

bor - der - town, ___ sat a   boy   and his   gui - tar, _____   and the
make   a   dime, ___ but   give   him   his   gui - tar, _____   and
saw   him 'round. ___ He   van - ished   like   the   breeze, ___   and they for -

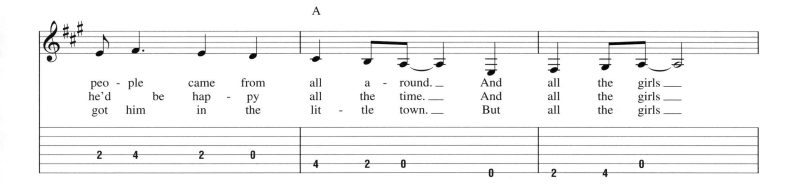

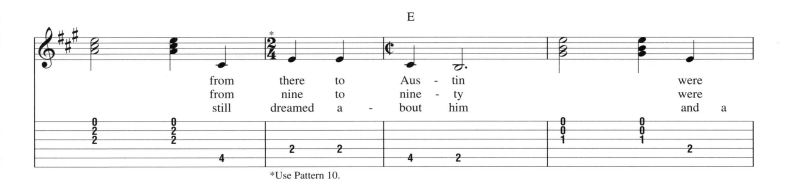

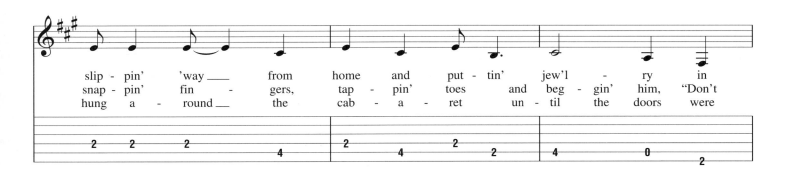

*Use Pattern 10.

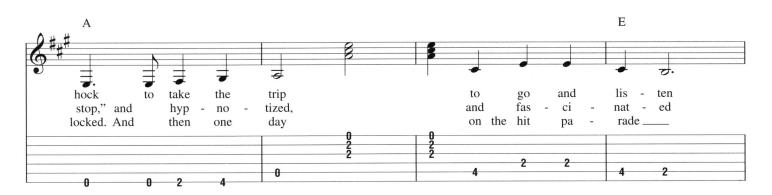

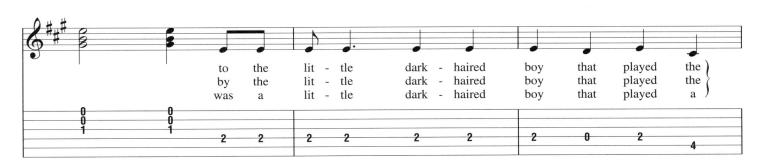

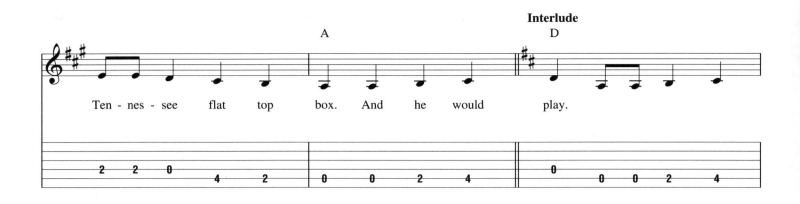

Ten - nes - see flat top box. And he would play.

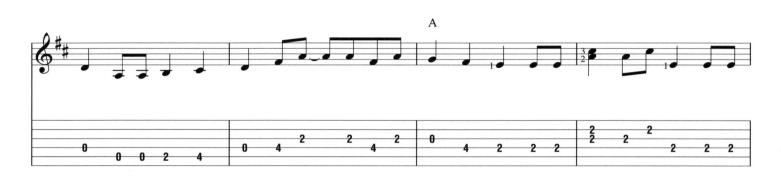

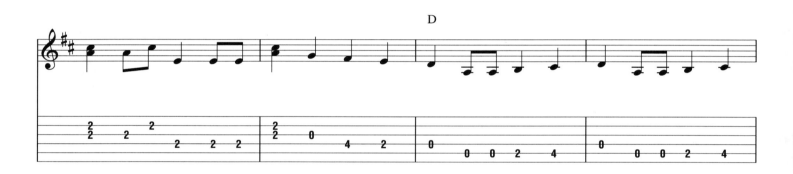

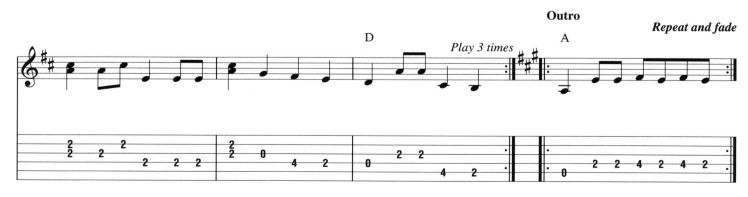

Understand Your Man

Words and Music by Johnny R. Cash

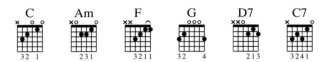

Strum Pattern: 4
Pick Pattern: 3

Verse
Moderately, in 2

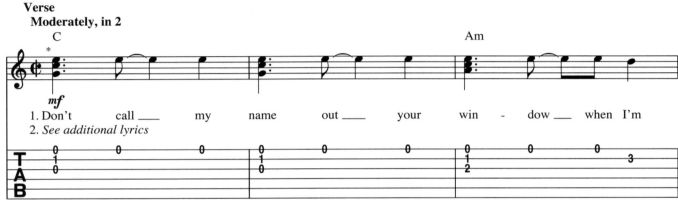

1. Don't call ___ my name out ___ your win - dow ___ when I'm
2. *See additional lyrics*

*Sung one octave lower.

leav - in', ___   I won't e - ven turn my head.

Don't ___ send your kin - folks ___ to   give me no

talk - in', _____ I'll be gone _____ like I said.

Bridge

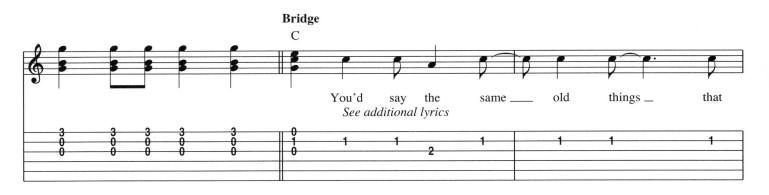

You'd say the same _____ old things _____ that
See additional lyrics

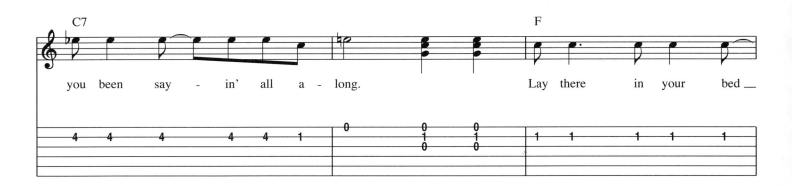

you been say - in' all a - long. Lay there in your bed _____

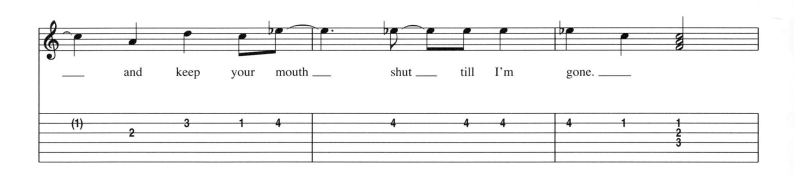

_____ and keep your mouth _____ shut _____ till I'm gone. _____

Don't give me that old _____ fa - mil - iar cry - in', cuss - in' moan.

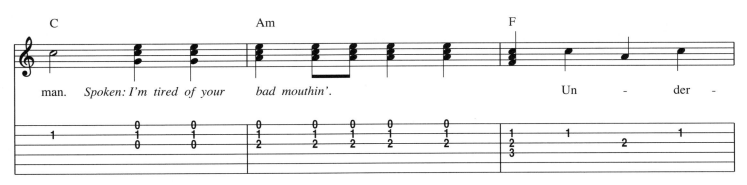

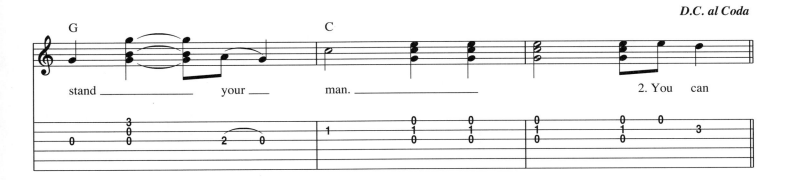

Additional Lyrics

2. You can give my other suit to the Salvation Army
   And ev'rything else I leave behind.
   I ain't takin' nothin' that'll slow down my travelin'
   While I'm untanglin' my mind.

Bridge I ain't gonna repeat what I said anymore,
   While I'm breathin' air that ain't been breathed before.
   I'll be as gone as a wild goose in winter,
   Then you'll understand your man.

What Is Truth?

Words and Music by John R. Cash

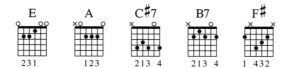

Strum Pattern: 3
Pick Pattern: 1, 3

Intro
Moderately, in 2

1.*Spoken: The

*Lyrics in italics are
spoken throughout.

% Verse

old man turned off   the   ra - di - o,   said, "Where did all of the old
2., 3., 4. See additional lyrics

songs   go?   Kids   sure   play   fun - ny   mu - sic   these   days,

and they play it in the strang - est ways." Said, "It looks to me like they've

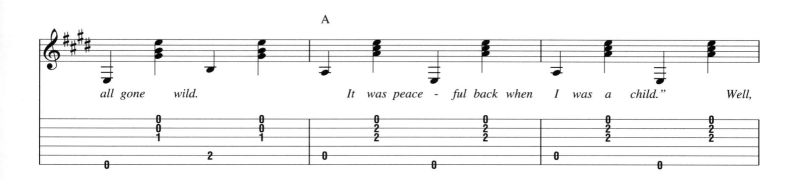

all gone wild. It was peace - ful back when I was a child." Well,

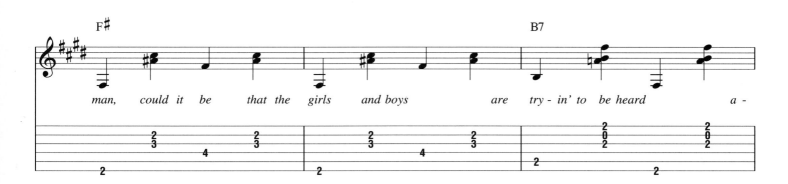

man, could it be that the girls and boys are try - in' to be heard a -

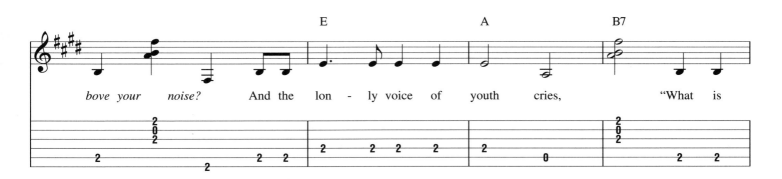

bove your noise? And the lon - ly voice of youth cries, "What is

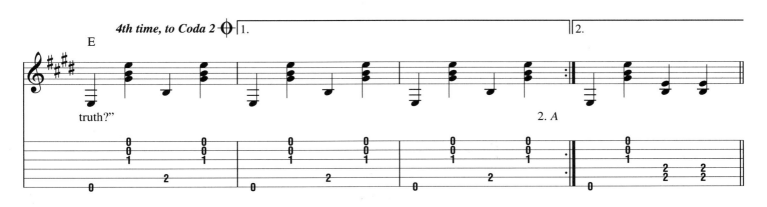

truth?"

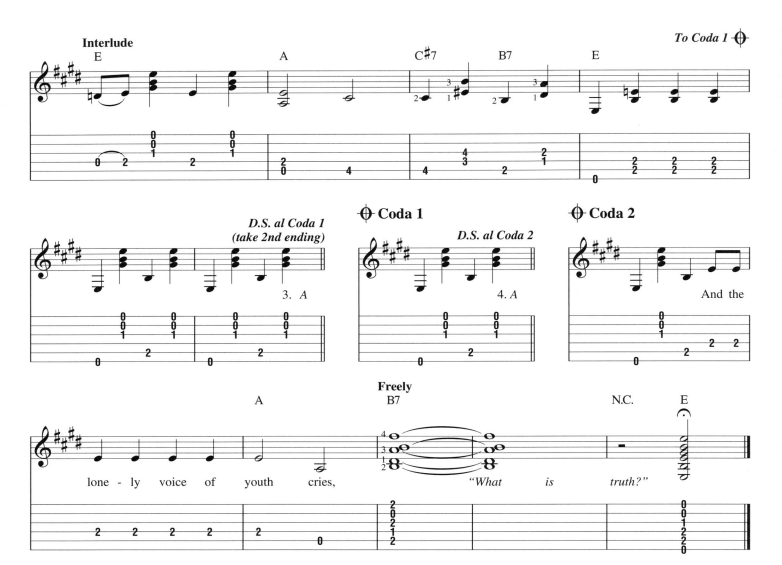

Additional Lyrics

2. *A little boy of three, sittin' on the floor,*
   Looks up and says, "Daddy, what is war?"
   Son, that's when people fight and die."
   The little boy of three says, "Daddy, why?"
   Young man of seventeen in Sunday school
   Bein' taught the golden rule,
   And by the time another year's gone around,
   It may be his turn to lay his life down.
   Can you blame the voice of youth for asking,
   "What is truth?"

3. *A young man sittin' on the witness stand,*
   The man with the book says, "Raise your hand.
   Repeat after me, I solemnly swear."
   The man looked down at his long hair.
   And although the young man solemnly swore,
   Nobody seemed to hear anymore,
   And it didn't really matter if the truth was there,
   It was the cut of his clothes and the length of his hair.
   And the lonely voice of youth cries,
   "What is truth?"

4. *A young girl dancin' to the latest beat*
   Has found new ways to move her feet.
   A young man speakin' in the city square
   Is tryin' to tell somebody that he cares.
   Yeah, the ones that you're callin' wild
   Are gonna be the leaders in a little while.
   This whole world's wakin' to a newborn day,
   And I solemnly swear that it'll be their way.
   You better help that voice of youth find
   What is truth.